So What Do We Do About Henry?

A Play

Charlotte Hastings

A SAMUEL FRENCH ACTING EDITION

SAMUELFRENCH-LONDON.CO.UK
SAMUELFRENCH.COM

Copyright © 1990 by Charlotte Hastings
All Rights Reserved

SO WHAT DO WE DO ABOUT HENRY? is fully protected under the copyright laws of the British Commonwealth, including Canada, the United States of America, and all other countries of the Copyright Union. All rights, including professional and amateur stage productions, recitation, lecturing, public reading, motion picture, radio broadcasting, television and the rights of translation into foreign languages are strictly reserved.

ISBN 978-0-573-11407-6

www.samuelfrench-london.co.uk

www.samuelfrench.com

FOR AMATEUR PRODUCTION ENQUIRIES

UNITED KINGDOM AND WORLD EXCLUDING NORTH AMERICA

plays@SamuelFrench-London.co.uk

020 7255 4302/01

Each title is subject to availability from Samuel French, depending upon country of performance.

CAUTION: Professional and amateur producers are hereby warned that *SO WHAT DO WE DO ABOUT HENRY?* is subject to a licensing fee. Publication of this play does not imply availability for performance. Both amateurs and professionals considering a production are strongly advised to apply to the appropriate agent before starting rehearsals, advertising, or booking a theatre. A licensing fee must be paid whether the title is presented for charity or gain and whether or not admission is charged.

The professional rights in this play are controlled by Samuel French Ltd, 52 Fitzroy Street, London, W1T 5JR.

No one shall make any changes in this title for the purpose of production. No part of this book may be reproduced, stored in a retrieval system, or transmitted in any form, by any means, now known or yet to be invented, including mechanical, electronic, photocopying, recording, videotaping, or otherwise, without the prior written permission of the publisher. No one shall upload this title, or part of this title, to any social media websites.

The right of Charlotte Hastings to be identified as author of this work has been asserted by her in accordance with Section 77 of the Copyright, Designs and Patents Act 1988

So What Do We Do About Henry?

First produced on BBC Radio 4 on 25th/27th October 1980, with the following cast of characters:

Elsie	Jane Knowles
Dino	Graham Faulkener
Henrietta	Dame Flora Robson
Meredith Gane	Sean Barrett
Mrs Morris	Margot Boyde
Admiral Featherstone	Timothy Bateson
Delia	Paula Tinker
Rupert Dominic*	Kenneth Barrow

The play was directed by **Graham Gauld**

* In this printed version of the play the character of Rupert Dominic is female

The action of the play takes place in a Cornish cottage on a clifftop, in a village a few miles from Plymouth

ACT I	A January evening
ACT II Scene 1	About a month later. 11am
Scene 2	About five weeks later. Morning
ACT III Scene 1	A month later. Late evening
Scene 2	June. Early evening

Time: the present

If it is preferred to perform the play in two acts, then the interval should occur after Act II, Scene 2

For Flora —
great actress, beloved friend

PRODUCTION NOTE

This play is intended to be a comedy. It makes no social comment nor conveys any message. It sets out to provide an amusing story for the "two-hour traffic of the stage". Therefore it depends especially on pace, and all the stage directions and movements of the actors have been worked out to this end. If companies will at least try out these instructions, it will be found that everyone is active with everyday things, and this, by combining movements with dialogue as shown, should have the desired effect.

The characters should not be over-exaggerated or played for farce. The Admiral is basically a gentleman, not a bully. His changing moods, from impatience to kindness, are clearly indicated. Dino is not a comic character; he is lazy and charming like many talented people and once under the influence of the business-like Rupert, starts to develop. Delia must not go over the top too much, or she will lose sympathy. Mrs Morris' pansy hat should not be grotesque. The gimmick is that she is *never*—whatever the occasion-seen without it! Above all, Henry is not, in fact, bossy or interfering. She is a strong-minded lady who has been used to a controlled and organized life.

It may not be possible to arrange a stage with three entrances. Therefore the curtains to bedroom and studio may mask small alcoves behind which the actors may wait to return on stage.

Many companies now prefer to work within two acts. If so, Act I may incorporate the two scenes of Act II, making a fairly long first act of three scenes. It has been arranged in the script that the actors quite naturally move most of the furniture and props into position for the next scene, and if these directions are followed, the individual scenes may be managed with only the briefest time for fall and rise of the curtain. Alternatively, a programme note may warn the audience that there will be a few minutes between Acts I and II, with the long main interval between Acts II and III.

Charlotte Hastings

ACT I

The interior of a Cornish cottage. An evening in January

In the back wall, there is a brick fireplace with a wide hearth and a shelf above with old china jugs, etc. L *of the hearth is a brown upholstered armchair. Opposite it,* R, *an antique high-backed armchair with bright but shabby green velvet upholstery.* L *of the wall by the fireplace, a small cupboard with an electric kettle on top and wall plug. The cupboard is practical; shelves inside hold a coffee filter and everything for making coffee. In the wall* L *of the fireplace a long floor-length chintz curtain hides a staircase to the bedrooms*

The door to the main part of the house is C *of the wall* R. *Above the door near the fireplace a tall dresser with drawers and a cupboard underneath. Three shelves hold books, a clutter of cups and saucers, a drawing-pad, etc.* C *of the wall* L *is a wide sash window (practical), with chintz curtains and a window seat with cushions and a valance to the floor. Below the window there is another floor-length chintz curtain, masking an entrance to the studio and garden*

The furniture is simple. R *below the main door a small trolley; above it a wall mirror and a row of hooks with two anoraks hanging.* C *a small gate-legged table with one flap down. There are rush-seated chairs at each end and a third chair up* L *between the curtain* C *and the window seat. On the window sill is a modern plug-in telephone with a very long cord. Everything is clean and bright but rather shabby*

When the CURTAIN *rises, a bright fire burns in the grate. A line is strung across above the fireplace with two tea-towels and a light sweater hung to air. The curtains are drawn across the window. Voices and laughter are heard off* C

Elsie (*off*) No, Dino ... ! No ... !

Elsie runs in C *laughing, a slim pretty Cornish girl of about twenty-five. She wears an attractive lacy bra and a trim tweed skirt which she is zipping up as she enters*

Dino (*off*) Elsie—!

He runs in C. *He is in his early thirties, very good-looking and with tremendous charm. He wears only a pair of bright coloured shorts*

—come back to bed!

Elsie takes a sweater from the line and puts it on

Elsie Tes five o'clock in the afternoon. And suppose that phone rings again.

Dino Take it off the hook. (*He goes behind her and puts his arms around her, kissing her neck*)
Elsie Stop it, can't you! I've got to get to work.
Dino It's hours to opening time.
Elsie I do other things besides pulling pints.
Dino (*tightening his hold*) I know.
Elsie (*struggling and laughing*) I told you, Dino! Stop it!

Loud knocking off R

Oh, damn—now there's someone at the door. You're not decent. I'll go——

The knocking is repeated

Henry (*calling off*) Dino! Dino ...!
Dino My God—it can't be. Henry ...!
Elsie Tes never your auntie. She's next week.
Henry (*calling off,*) Dino!
Dino By the sound of it, she's *now*.
Elsie You get upstairs and put your pants on. (*Calling*) I'm coming—all right, I'm coming.

She hurries off R

Dino hurries off through the curtain C

Confused voices off R

Henry		Good-evening ...
Elsie	(*together*)	Why—tes Vicar ...
Merry		Hallo, Elsie ...

Elsie returns, holding the door open

Elsie Through here—that's right ...

Henry enters R. *She is a slender, sophisticated woman in her fifties, with a deceptively gentle manner, shrewd eyes and a natural warmth. She wears a well-cut dark suit, no hat and has a fur coat draped over her shoulders. She carries a handbag, is wearing gloves and is very slightly out of breath*

Meredith (Merry) Gane enters behind her, carrying her expensive leather suitcase. He is a dark pleasant young man, about thirty-five, wearing his clerical suit under a short sheepskin coat. He puts the case on the trolley

Henry takes a quick glance round the room and holds out her hand

Henry (*smiling*) Elsie—is it?
Elsie And you must be Dino's auntie. Come you away in, my dear, and get warm.

Merry comes forward and takes her coat from her shoulders

Merry May I take this ...

Act I

Henry Oh, thank you, yes. (*She comes to the table, puts her handbag down and stands taking off her gloves*)

Merry puts the coat on the trolley

Forgive me while I get my breath back. How many steps up to that path?
Elsie (*laughing*) It seems much more because of the steep slope. There's only thirty-four.
Henry Thirty-four ...!
Elsie And path bends right round the house. If you go out the front door and turn right, I can go to that window and look left and see you walking right down to the end. Merry—how did you come to meet Miss Henry ...
Merry I called at the station to collect some books and found a lady in distress.
Henry I did phone a couple of times from the call box but——
Elsie Oh, I'm so sorry. We—we must have—(*pausing*)—been busy ...

Dino tumbles in C, *now wearing an old but flamboyant silk dressing-gown and sandals*

Dino Henry, darling! (*He crosses and takes both her hands*) Some absolutely unforgiveable mix-up! The fourteenth. Next week ...!
Henry The fourth. Today.
Dino I grovel and abase myself. Well, we may have missed the red carpet, but welcome—most warmly welcome—to Gull Cottage. Be happy here for as long as you like to stay. (*He kisses her hands*)
Henry (*drily*) Thank you, Dino. Very prettily said.
Dino And forgive my not coming to meet you.
Henry Your Vicar deputized very ably. (*She sits* R *above the table, putting her handbag on the floor*)
Dino Bless him, he always does. Merry, can I get you a drink?
Merry No—no, thank you. (*Glancing at his wrist-watch*) There's the Parish Meeting at seven. And the Chairman turns purple if we start late. (*He crosses to Henry*) Goodbye, Miss Ellis. Glad to have been of service.
Henry Thank you. (*Giving him her hand*) I'm most grateful.
Merry And if you're staying, I hope we'll meet again.
Henry If we do, most people call me Miss Henry.
Merry They call me Merry.

They shake hands. He waves across to Dino and Elsie

See you ...
Elsie } (*together*) I'll see you out ...
Dino } 'Bye, Merry.

Elsie and Merry exit R

Dino Did you have a grisly journey?
Henry Perfect until I arrived here. Then we met another car in a long lane, and some quite unreasonable person tried to make the Vicar back.
Dino Did Merry say who it was?

Elsie returns

Elsie Now you just let your auntie sit and rest a bit. And I'll make her a good hot cup of coffee—with a smidgeon of rum in it. (*She crosses* C *and plugs in the kettle*)
Henry What a magnificent idea! Your Vicar—a *very* pleasant young man.
Dino He's new. Finding things a bit hard, I'm afraid.
Henry I wouldn't have thought——
Dino His predecessor was an ancient silver-haired saint, who lived vaguely and happily somewhere above the bright blue sky——
Elsie You stop talking nonsense, and take your auntie's things upstairs. (*She fetches the case and coat from the trolley, and gives him the case*) And here—(*handing the coat*)—be careful. And make yourself civilized before you come back.

Dino laughs, kisses the tip of her nose and goes out C *through the curtain*

Elsie opens the fireside cupboard and brings out a small tray with coffee filter, packet of coffee, a mug, small bottle of rum, etc. This does not interrupt the dialogue

Henry Elsie, if it's not convenient, I could find a hotel for a few days.
Elsie Bless you, no. He hasn't painted your room yet, but it's all cleaned ready and we'll soon pick up the clean sheets from Lucy Morris. She does them for me in the machine. (*She brings the tray to the table and spoons coffee into the filter*) And there's a little bathroom back of the kitchen. 'Tisn't grand, but everything works——

The kettle boils. She takes the filter over to it

—and emptied three times a week. (*She fills the filter and returns to the table*) There, me dear. We'll just let that drip through. Are you hungry?
Henry Thank you. I had something on the train.
Elsie Oh, those bits of plastic rubbish. I wouldn't insult my teeth. I could soon whip you up an omelette before I go down to *Lobster*.
Henry Thank you, but please don't bother. Who or what is "Lobster"?
Elsie *The Lobster Pot*. Our local. I work there.
Henry And live here?
Elsie Mostly. Sometimes I stay down with Delia. She's my sister. She has the shop. With Arthur.
Henry Her husband?
Elsie (*laughing*) Oh, she haven't a husband. Only Arthur—he's rising four. Sometimes I give them a hand. They're neither of them so sharp as you might say. (*She pours coffee into the mug and adds a tot of rum*) There you be, my dear. Try that.
Dino (*off*) Elsie! Elsie! Where're my jeans?
Elsie (*calling*) You dropped 'em. You find 'em. (*To Henry*) You have to talk firm to him, see?
Henry I see that you work at a pub, help with a baby—and a shop—and then cherish my charming but idle nephew. Why?
Elsie (*simply*) Tes his masterpiece.
Henry His what?

Act I   5

Elsie (*perching on the edge of the table*) That great picture he's painting. When that's finished, we'll all be right.
Henry I see. And when is this great undertaking likely to be finished?
Elsie Who knows? He busies away at it for weeks and then suddenly he'll scrat all the paint off and start again.
Henry Where does he work? (*She finishes her coffee and empties the filter into her mug*)
Elsie Studio through there. (*Indicating the curtain* L) It's a Nissen really, but it's got a door to garden, and Willy Flagg took out one end and put in all windows. And he can plug the phone in there, so you might say he's self-contained.
Henry Is he working at the moment?
Elsie I'm not sure. Sometimes he just sits writing his little poems for Arthur. They really are lovely, Miss Henry, would you like to see them sometime?
Henry Do you know, I think I would. (*She finishes her coffee*) Thank you, Elsie. That was magnificent.
Elsie But you did ought to eat something. Dino comes to pick me up and we have our bite there. But you wouldn't want to do that—I know! Lucy Morris brought up some of her pasties yesterday. I could warm them up—and make a fresh brew of coffee.
Henry Now, I think that would be just right.
Elsie (*going to the curtain* C *and calling*) Dino! Could you eat a pasty with your auntie?
Dino (*off*) Surely.

Elsie bustles back to the table and collects things on to the tray

Elsie 'Twon't take above a minute under the grill.
Henry (*getting up*) And while you're doing that, could I go up and see my room?
Elsie Course you can. Straight up and it's opposite the stairs.

Henry goes out C *through the curtain*

Elsie takes the tea-towels from the line above the fireplace and drapes them over her shoulder

Dino enters C, *now tidy in jeans and a thick roll-neck sweater*

Elsie lifts the tray and turns to face him

(*Quietly*) You didn't tell me she was a lady.
Dino (*laughing*) No, love. She's what used to be called a gentlewoman.
Elsie (*tartly*) Then you get and find a proper tablecloth. No need to let her think we're savages.

She goes out R

Dino goes to the dresser and takes a red checked tablecloth from the top drawer. He spreads it on the table, returns to the dresser and fetches a bottle of wine and two glasses to the table. He feels in his pockets and produces a corkscrew

Henry enters C through a curtain

Henry It's a charming little room. All angles—and what a superb view.
Dino Do you know, I think I was quite clever not to paint it. Now you can choose your own colour.
Henry (*crossing back to the table*) That's what I call turning something to your own advantage. Dino—might I ask you? Could I have my bed sent down—and I have one or two small bits and pieces—personal things?
Dino Send for anything you like, old love. We'll wedge everything in somewhere.
Henry Oh, thank you ... (*She moves to the chair* R)

Dino goes behind her and seats her

Dino And as this is an occasion, I thought we might crack a bottle.

He inserts the corkscrew. Henry reaches out and looks at the label

Henry Forgive my asking, but can we afford to crack many bottles like this?
Dino (*solemnly*) Lady, all dues are bonded. Let your conscience rest.
Henry On what?
Dino Actually, a couple of sketches for early tourists, and a two-colour poster for the AGM of the Women's Institute. (*He removes the corkscrew, fills the glasses and pushes one towards her*) O taste and see that the Lord is good!

He raises his glass to her. They both drink

Henry Mm. Whatever do you charge your clients!
Dino (*laughing*) Just the price of the bottle.
Henry Dino!
Dino Henry, old love—this is *today*. Tomorrow you and I could be a drift of grey smoke against a blue sky. (*Thoughtfully*) I could paint that. The dark smoke—the pale blue. And I'd call it "The After Life". (*He laughs and sits down* L *opposite her*) But this is the real life, isn't it, old love. What more? A loaf of bread, a jug of wine——
Henry (*quietly*) And Elsie.
Dino And Elsie.
Henry (*still quiet*) Why don't you marry her?
Dino No. It wouldn't be fair.
Henry Why not?
Dino One day she'll meet someone who can give her a good life. Money, and clothes. And lots of gorgeous fat babies like Botticelli cherubs.
Henry Perhaps she doesn't want the money or the clothes. (*Drily*) Would you find it so difficult to provide the Botticelli babies?
Dino (*laughing*) The difficulty there is not to.
Henry But——

Dino reaches across and fills up her glass

Dino (*deliberately*) How's old sister Sabrina these days? Still filling a single bed with two people?

Act I

Elsie enters R *with the tray now containing the pasties, re-filled filter jug, mugs, plates, cutlery etc.*

Elsie There you are, my 'andsomes. (*She puts the tray on the table, and goes to the pegs* R *for her anorak and returns* C *putting it on, talking all the time*) I'll ring Lucy Morris as soon as I get in, and tell her you'll pick up the sheets on the way down. And put a log on the fire before you leave.

She gives him a quick kiss. He returns it together with a playful smack on her bottom

Now you just behave yourself and look after your auntie. 'Bye, Miss Henry ... (*She hurries to the door* R *and turns*) And Dino—you'd better tell her about Vulcan.

She runs out R. *The door slams*

Dino sits back in his chair. During the next scene, they eat their snack and drink their coffee and wine

Dino And now, my old love, it appears that our reverent and recently deceased uncle has deposited you right up the effluent creek without adequate means of propulsion.

Henry (*drily*) You *could* put it like that.

Dino Charles phoned me. As the family solicitor he thought I should know. It seems almost every penny goes to charity.

Henry Something called the Gravistonian Research and Archaeological Trust. (*She picks up her handbag and puts it on the table, takes out spectacles and a folded paper. She puts on her spectacles and opens the paper*)

Dino Henry, I can't believe it. You've been with him—organized his life—for what—thirty years? He just couldn't——

Henry (*reading*) "To my niece Henrietta Margaret Ellis—who is already in receipt of certain small emoluments—and who has most efficiently shared with me many years of travel and gracious living——"

Dino Yes——?

Henry (*quietly*) "I leave the sum of five hundred pounds and my grateful thanks——"

Dino WHAT——!

Henry holds up a warning hand and reads on

Henry "—also the remaining four bottles of the Trenellenburg brandy which I trust she is sufficiently civilized not to drink after any meal which has included shellfish." (*She refolds the paper and returns it to her bag*)

Dino That's an insult '!

Henry Oh, no dear. Wait till you taste it.

Dino The old bastard! Naturally, *I* didn't expect anything—but is there nothing—absolutely *nothing*—for *anyone* else in the family?

Henry (*cheerfully*) Not a bloodstained copper. (*She takes off her spectacles and puts them beside her plate*)

Dino My God—I bet they're all furious! I can just see them. Wallace—no, wait... (*He gets up and goes to the dresser for the drawing-pad and comes back to the table, feeling in his pockets*) Pencil—pencil—why have I never got a pencil... (*He finds one, flattens the pad on the table and begins sketching with swift sure strokes*) Wallace here—looking like Cromwell in a black mood—just bring his eyebrows down a bit—and Emily—netting up her little mouth in disapproving wrinkles. And sister Sabrina—poor Sab—too tense, too thin—and all the jangly bracelets. (*He pushes the sketch over*)

Henry Dino—all in a few strokes. It's brilliant. (*Slowly*) It needs a caption.
Dino What are—what was that phrase—"certain small emoluments"?
Henry (*quietly*) A few small investments. And a little annuity. I'm selling my car and most of my jewellery. Charles said——
Dino (*abruptly*) Charles said "Miss Henry has a little pocket money. What she needs is a home."

Henry does not answer

By God—there's your caption. (*Scribbling*) All wetting their pants and wailing "So what do we do about Henry." (*He holds up the drawing*)
Henry (*shortly*) It is not contingent upon anyone to do anything.
Dino Oh, come on. Who staked Wallace's first venture? Who guaranteed Emily's mortgage? How much went into Sab's agency—and if that shows tuppence on the balance sheet they think it's a good year.
Henry I think I can manipulate sufficient income to fit in somewhere——
Dino Not with a selfish mini-tycoon, a holy-holy do-gooder or—let's face it—a near nymphomaniac. So——(*He crumples the sketch and throws it into the fireplace*)—what you need for the immediate moment, old love, is a breathing space.
Henry (*gently*) So you sent me a postcard. (*She opens her bag and brings out a postcard. Reading*) "Henry, darling, come to us at Gull Cottage. Two up and two down and primitive. Me—and Elsie who is beautiful as the morning star and gormless in everything except bed. Dino. PS. Send time and I'll meet train. PPS. Elsie is occasionally vociferous. Some nights you may have to knock on the wall." (*She looks up. Quietly*) What did I ever do for you?
Dino You can't have forgotten. When I was chucked out of University——
Henry You were *not* chucked out of University. You left of your own accord because you wanted to go to France and study art.
Dino So my parents chucked me out instead. And you sent me fifty pounds and a one-way ticket to Paris. And said "Pay me back when you sell your first real picture."
Henry (*quietly*) So you'd better get on and finish masterpiece.
Dino Masterpiece? (*Laughing*) You mustn't listen to Elsie.
Henry But you *are* working on one?
Dino Off and on, love. On and off.
Henry When may I see it?
Dino (*refilling his glass*) Now, if you like.
Henry Now? Where is it?
Dino Studio. (*Nodding* L) Through there.

Act I

Henry puts on her spectacles and gets up

Henry Come and show me.
Dino I feel lazy. Have a look for yourself.

Henry goes through the curtain L

(*Calling*) Light switch just inside. Mind that green metal thing—a bit further on——

A light switch clicks on off L

Henry (*off*) Dino ...!

She comes back through the curtain

What a mountain of stuff! Don't you ever sell *anything*?
Dino Only if I think it's good enough.
Henry Where's masterpiece?
Dino Right at the end.

Henry goes off behind the curtain

Dino leans back, drinking his wine. He is suddenly tense. A pause

Henry (*off*) Dino! It's marvellous!

Dino jerks round

(*Off*) The whole wall. A complete village.

She re-appears through the curtain

Little houses and trees—and people—and the colour! You didn't say it was a mural——
Dino Henry——
Henry It must have taken months. The whole thing is real—bustling—it's alive——
Dino Henry——
Henry I must look again.
Dino (*loudly*) Henry——

She turns

That isn't masterpiece.
Henry Not——
Dino It's Arthur's Wall.
Henry Arthur's——?
Dino Elsie's nephew. I look after him sometimes—when the girls are busy. He's a poor little bundle—doesn't talk much—and he muddles and bobbles about. So I started it just to amuse him and keep him quiet. Now he sits and looks at it for hours—and mutters away in his own jargon—like a little buzz-saw.
Henry If that isn't masterpiece—where *is* it?
Dino On the big easel. At the end.
Henry Right!

She goes back through the curtain

A pause

(*Off*) You *did* say—big easel ...
Dino Right at the end.

Another pause

Henry returns L

Henry It *has* to be a joke.
Dino Deadly serious. It's called Abstract Ambition.
Henry I'd call it——
Dino Call it what you like, old love. It entirely depends on how you see it.
Henry All I can see is a plain white canvas—with two blue lines and one red—curving up from left to right.
Dino Well, ambition should curve up—or should it? Perhaps tomorrow I'll put in three yellow lines curving down.
Henry And that—piece—next to it? Three amorphous coloured blobs——
Dino Traffic Lights.
Henry All blurred——
Dino (*laughing*) It must have been a foggy day.
Henry There has to be something *normal*.

She goes out L *again*

Dino laughs and drinks his wine

(*Off*) Ah—this is better ...

She enters carrying two small pictures about eight inches square

Little landscapes. (*Turning them over*) "View over the Ancient Hills". "Message before Sunset". Charming.
Dino (*scornfully*) Picture postcards. You see them every day.
Henry Then they should be saleable.

She props them on the window seat and goes off L *again*

Dino Henry, do stop rattling and popping about with handfuls of rubbish. It's getting exhausting ...
Henry You should have come and shown me properly. Some of this stuff must have been here for years. Oh—I've found a nude——

Dino gets up suddenly

Henry comes back carrying a large oblong framed canvas, holding it in front of her and studying it intently

"The Morning Star". (*She looks up at him. Gently*) Elsie ...

He nods. She looks back at the picture

(*Quietly*) You're right. She *is* beautiful.

Dino takes the picture from her and slips it behind the curtain

Act I

Dino That's enough for this evening. Come and sit down. Tomorrow we'll——
Henry Just one more—right at the top. It looks intriguing ...

She goes back into the studio

Dino Henry—*please*!

There is a crash

Henry (*off*) Come and help me! Dino ... !
Dino Oh, hell ...

He goes through the curtain. More bumps and crashes

(*Off*) Careful—you'll fall. Watch out——!

A thud. Henry yelps. They return. Henry is limping and has a large smudge of dust on her right cheek. She is firmly clutching a canvas about three feet square

Are you all right ... ?
Henry Of course, I'm all right. (*She holds the picture in front of her, intent*) Just look at this!

Dino looks over her shoulder

Dino (*laughing*) "Old Polaris".
Henry "Old Polaris" ... ?
Dino The absolute ultimate deterrent. Cornwall's own private and personal atomic weapon.
Henry (*quietly*) Admiral Featherstone.
Dino That highlight could be—(*suddenly*)—what to you mean—Admiral Featherstone? You haven't met——
Henry (*still intent on the picture*) This evening. I backed his car.
Dino You *what* ... !
Henry Did he sit for this?
Dino Certainly not. He was in the pub—arguing with someone. Probably poor Merry Gane—it usually is. I made a sketch and finished it from memory.
Henry You know you've painted two pictures here.
Dino One. A fairly competent study of a belligerent old basket.
Henry Yes. And then one looks again. And you've caught the other side of his character. This is a sad and lonely man.
Dino Henry—did you really back his car?
Henry It was blocking the lane.
Dino Tell me. (*He takes the picture from her*) Tell me now ...
Henry We were nearly at the end and he came roaring up and shouted at the Vicar to back. I told him not to, of course. Then the Admiral got out and came to the window and bullied the Vicar quite disgracefully.
Dino So ... ?
Henry So then *I* got out and went to the Admiral's car, and backed it round the corner out of the way.

Dino You do realize you may have started World War Three?
Henry Then I shall certainly not be the one to surrender. This—*naval person*—who *does* he think he is?
Dino Didn't Merry tell you?
Henry Just said he was an important landowner. On all the Parish, Rural and County Councils.
Dino He is also the Vicar's Churchwarden.
Henry Oh, no! What have I done! Will there be repercussions?
Dino Probably a small crucifixion. Private, of course. But nonetheless effective.
Henry I shall call on the Vicar tomorrow and most humbly ask his pardon. (*She takes the picture from him, props it on the window seat, and crosses* C *behind the table, taking off her glasses. She turns to face him*) Dino, I have to say this whether you like it or not. I think you have a talent which, with work and discipline—might well be important. And what are you doing about it? Apparently nothing...

Dino laughs and comes C *behind the table*

Dino Do you know you've got a ruddy great smudge across your face? (*He takes her face in his hand*)
Henry Now, Dino...
Dino (*laughing*) Shut up and stand still. (*Holding her chin firmly, he tilts her face, dips a paper napkin in a wineglass and wipes the smudge from her face*) There—that's restored your beauty. (*Looking at her upturned face*) You know something, old Henry? You have very good bones. (*He lets her go, screws up the tissue and stuffs it in a wineglass*) And now I'm going to rush down to *The Lobster*. (*He goes to the peg for his anorak and puts it on, talking all the time*) You'll be all right, won't you? Logs for fire. kettle if you want more coffee. No TV, I'm afraid, but the radio's working. And there should be books (*waving vaguely*)—round and about. We'll be back about eleven——(*He turns* R *to the door*)
Henry (*suddenly*) Dino—wait—you've forgotten to tell me—something called Vulcan——
Dino Oh, God...! (*He strikes his forehead with the flat of his hand*) That green metal monster—behind the curtain——

Henry goes and moves the curtain aside and looks in

—boiler/generator thing—for water and lights.
Henry What do I need to know?
Dino He's temperamental. Sometimes he acts up.
Henry (*grimly*) Does he indeed? How?
Dino First he clanks and groans, and then the lights flicker—sometimes it's all right—but mostly they go out...
Henry What do I do then?
Dino There's a hammer hanging up beside him. Give him two or three socking great bangs and everything will be all right.
Henry Suppose it isn't?
Dino It mostly is. Don't panic. He's been quiet for quite a while.

Henry Is it remotely possible he might blow up altogether?
Dino If it does, it'll only knock out the main fuse. Look love, I must get in before Willy Flagg——
Henry Who is Willy Flagg?
Dino Keeps local garage. And has a roving eye which is beginning to settle too frequently in Elsie's direction.
Henry You can surely trust Elsie . . .
Dino Implicitly. I wouldn't trust Willy Flagg with a cow's eyelash.

He hurries off R. *The door bangs*

Henry returns C *to the table, picks up the filter and checks it is empty, then goes and plugs in the kettle. She puts a log on the fire. The fireglow comes up. She pauses, then picks up the crumpled cartoon sketch. She returns to the table, where she smooths out the sketch and looks at it. She folds it neatly and puts it in her handbag, together with her glasses. She looks thoughtfully round the room, goes to the dresser and switches on the radio. Soft background music. She looks along the books, then goes back to the table and spoons coffee into the filter. The kettle boils. She takes the filter over and fills it, switches off the kettle, goes back to the table and sits down* L *facing the door* R

The sound of the door opening. Mrs Morris enters R. *She is a plump country woman in her sixties, sometimes grim in manner but basically kind. She wears a tweed skirt, a brown leather jacket and a round black hat with a brim, trimmed with a wreath of improbable pansies. She carries an oblong brown paper parcel, and has a large handbag hooked over her arm*

Mrs Morris I'm Mrs Morris. I've brought the sheets.
Henry But how did you——?
Mrs Morris Got my own key. I'm in and out to help Elsie. Times she's on double shifts, she needs it.
Henry But Dino was supposed to—and he hasn't had time.
Mrs Morris Elsie phoned me as soon as she got in. I said "I'm not waiting for him." Time he remembered, his auntie'd still be sleeping in blankets next Christmas. (*She puts the parcel and her bag on the trolley and comes to the table*) So I come up straightaway.
Henry It's extremely kind of you—at least a couple of miles from the village—on a cold night.
Mrs Morris Tes all right. I've got the Mini. Would that coffee be hot?
Henry I'll get another cup——

She starts to get up, but Mrs Morris goes to the dresser, switches off the radio and brings a cup and saucer. She sits down R *opposite Henry. Henry pours coffee*

Do you take milk?
Mrs Morris Only with instant. Helps to cover the taste. (*She sips coffee and nods*) Not bad. Mind, her Ladyship always used to say there's only one way to make proper coffee. In an earthenware jug, properly warmed——
Henry —two heaped tablespoons of freshly ground beans to a pint of absolutely boiling water——

Mrs Morris — good pinch of salt ——
Henry (*laughing*) — and a tablespoon of cold water to clear it!
Mrs Morris Her Ladyship used eggshells. But 'twouldn't be my way. After all, why waste an egg?
Henry Why, indeed. Who is her Ladyship?
Mrs Morris Was. Gone these ten years. I was up at the house with them for twenty. Her and the Admiral.
Henry Oh. His wife.
Mrs Morris Bless you — no. His mother. Rattling round the sea in battle-ships, he never sat still long enough to get married. (*She raises her cup in both hands, eyeing Henry amusedly over the rim*) Backed his car, didn't you?
Henry (*annoyed*) For goodness' sake! I've only been here a few hours.
Mrs Morris Long enough. If you went down to *Lobster* now, I reckon you'd be cheered.
Henry It's too bad of Dino...
Mrs Morris 'Tweren't Dino.
Henry Surely not the Vicar...
Mrs Morris Nor him neither. Willy Flagg were there. In the lane.
Henry I certainly didn't see him.
Mrs Morris Well, he'd hardly show himself, would he? Behind hedge, checking on his snares.
Henry (*laughing*) Oh. Poaching.
Mrs Morris Partial to a nice rabbit pie, is Willy. Said you proper told the Admiral.
Henry I didn't like the way he treated the Vicar.
Mrs Morris Oh, Vicar's used to it. He's got some new-sounding ways, but we're getting to know him. He's a kind enough boy and no fool for all he's so quiet. If it came to a real tangle with the Admiral, you might be surprised who'd win.
Henry (*grimly*) I hope I'm there to see.
Mrs Morris Admiral makes a lot of noise, but it's more puff than blow. He's lonely, living up by himself at the Dower.
Henry Dower...?
Mrs Morris Dower House. Sold the big place when her Ladyship died. Used to be half a dozen of us and more. Now he's got me two hours each morning, and five hours for a good going-through once a month.
Henry He should count himself lucky.
Mrs Morris I'll put those sheets on for you if you like. (*She gets up and goes to the trolley*)
Henry Thank you — I can manage...
Mrs Morris 'Tis no bother (*She turns, holding the parcel*) Not much of a little room, even if he do get round to painting it. He'd rather paint his pictures.
Henry He does paint rather well.
Mrs Morris Did I say he didn't? Did one of Willy Flagg outside his garage. So lifelike you could smell the grease. Well, I'll get on.

Act I   15

A knock at the door off R

Henry Now who——
Mrs Morris I'll go.

She goes out R

Henry (*calling*) It can only be for Dino. Just say he isn't here.

Voices are heard off R. *Mrs Morris comes back*

Mrs Morris It's the Admiral.
Henry I told you. Dino isn't here.
Mrs Morris He doesn't want Dino. He wants you.
Henry But——
Admiral (*off*) I won't keep her a moment...

Mrs Morris goes out R

Henry suddenly jumps up, goes quickly to the windowseat and turns the Admiral's picture face down. She goes back to the L *end of table just as* ...

The Admiral strides in R *with Mrs Morris behind him. He is a tall, handsome, commanding man in his sixties, silver hair, tanned face. He wears cavalry twill trousers, a short fawn leather coat lined with sheepskin, and carries a white envelope*

Admiral Good-evening. Miss Ellis, isn't it? Miss Henrietta Ellis. Be obliged if you'd spare me a moment.
Mrs Morris (*quietly*) I'll do the sheets. (*She crosses* C)
Admiral (*looking at his wrist-watch*) If you're finished when I go, Mrs Morris, I could give you a lift down.
Mrs Morris Thank you, sir. I've got the Mini.

She goes out C *through the curtain*

The Admiral comes C *to the table*

Admiral I brought a note in case you weren't in. Shan't need it now. (*He puts the note in his breast pocket*)

They look at each other across the table

Aren't you going to ask me to sit down?
Henry (*gently*) Are you planning to stay?
Admiral (*quietly*) I *did* say a few minutes.

They look at each other for a second. Then Henry makes a gesture towards a chair. He sits down. She sits opposite

If you've got Lucy Morris helping, you couldn't do better. Clacks like a dishwasher, but never really gossips, if you know what I mean.
Henry (*briefly*) Yes.
Admiral Known her for years. Used to be with us at the big house. Tell you that, did she?

Henry Yes.
Admiral Had to sell it when the old lady died. Damned Death Duties. Call it Inheritance Tax now, but it amounts to the same thing. Legalized Robbery with Violence.

Henry does not speak

Been turned into a school. One of those so-called progressive places. Turning out a lot of little mud-faced Marxists. (*Suddenly angry*) God knows why the Socialists keep on about destroying the rich——
Henry Admiral——
Admiral If they'd trouble to read the Finance Act they'd realize the Government is doing it very efficiently for them.
Henry Admiral——

He pauses. Again they look at each other for a second

I do not imagine you came here just to discuss your survival problems.
Admiral I'll pick you up tomorrow outside the shop. Eleven o'clock.
Henry I *beg* your pardon——
Admiral Run you up to the house for a glass of sherry. Can offer you a reasonable Amontillado. And Mrs Morris' little savoury biscuits—nuts and wheatflour or something. Go very well with a nice bit of Brie.
Henry Admiral—are you asking——
Admiral (*jumping up*) Damn it, you stupid woman! I'm trying to apologize!

A pause

Henry (*very quiet*) Have you already apologized to the Vicar?
Admiral Gane? (*Brusquely*) Man's a mouse.
Henry Even a mouse needs a chance.
Admiral Why?
Henry Apparently his predecessor was something between Father Christmas and Gentle Jesus meek and mild——
Admiral Good man, Wainwright. My type. Liked him a lot.
Henry And along comes someone young and enthusiastic——
Admiral And turning everything sides to middle. D'you know he's trying to make us accept that—that new abomination of words. The Alternative Service!
Henry Oh. Well, I do admit I'm not very happy with that, but——
Admiral I should damn well hope not. The fellow's doing nothing more nor less than castrating the prayer book—laying down the law——
Henry (*Gently*) I thought you said he was a mouse.

The Admiral stops dead. He looks at her once again

Admiral Well, whatever he is, he doesn't rate with me.
Henry I'm sure you could see the Bishop and arrange for a replacement.

They measure glances again

Admiral I'll see you at eleven. Don't be late.

He strides to the door R

Act I

Henry Admiral...

He turns in the doorway

(*Gently*) If I'm not there by quarter past, I'm not coming.

He pauses a second, then nods

Admiral *Touché.*

He goes out R. *The outer door shuts*

Mrs Morris returns C *carefully folding the brown paper*

Mrs Morris I thought I'd wait till he'd gone. Don't worry. I didn't listen. (*She goes to the trolley and puts the brown paper in her handbag*) I've made the bed. The blankets are clean. And I switched on the little fire.
Henry Thank you.
Mrs Morris (*moving back* C) But I still think it's not what you're used to. And that poor little wedge of a bathroom downstairs——
Henry (*sharply*) My dear Mrs Morris, I once spent twelve months in a Mexican hut. The bathroom was two holes in the ground—one with a bowl for washing, and one with a bucket for everything else.
Mrs Morris We did hear as you'd travelled a bit. Digging things up, wasn't it? Bricks and old bones.
Henry Plenty of those.
Mrs Morris Like to come down and talk to us about them?
Henry How do you mean—talk...
Mrs Morris Women's Institute. Every third Tuesday. 'Twould make a nice change from jam-making and flower-arranging. No-one tells me how to make jam, and the place for flowers is in the garden.
Henry (*laughing*) I'll certainly think about it.
Mrs Morris Take your time and tell me. I'm secretary. (*She turns up* R)
Henry Mrs Morris...

Mrs Morris turns

Do I understand that you sometimes—oblige?
Mrs Morris If you mean cleaning, say so. How else would I pay my bills?
Henry Perhaps you'd give me a hand with my room. Not for about three weeks. I'm having some things sent down from London.
Mrs Morris Let me know and I'll fit it in.
Henry What do you charge?
Mrs Morris Three pound an hour normal. People I like—by arrangement.
Henry (*smiling*) What arrangement would you suggest for me?

Mrs Morris considers her for a second

Mrs Morris One-seventy-five to start with, and see how we go on.
Henry Mrs Morris, we have a deal.

Mrs Morris nods and takes her handbag from the trolley

Mrs Morris I'll see myself out.

She goes out R. *The door shuts*

Henry collects everything on to the tray and goes out R

There is a loud groaning and clanking sound off L. *The Lights begin to flicker madly on and off*

Henry (*off* R) Oh—NO ... !

She appears in the doorway R, *just as the Lights go out completely, leaving the stage in darkness except for the glow of the fire. The groaning and clanking continues, Henry runs across* C *bumps into the table and yelps*

Oh, damn—*damn*! Why isn't there a torch ...

She goes through the curtain L

The sounds continue. Suddenly three loud clangs of a hammer on metal. The Lights come on again, flickering wildly for a second, then return to full

Henry enters L *rubbing her knee*

For goodness' sake ... ! (*She loses her balance, grabs the window seat for support and knocks the Admiral's picture to the floor. She picks it up*) And as for you ... (*She goes to put it back in the studio, then puts it back upright on the window seat, again rubbing her knee. She takes the telephone on its long cord to the table, where she sits down. She dials and waits. On the phone*) Brander? ... Miss Henrietta. Is Mr Charles available? ... Thank you, yes. (*She waits*) Charles dear! It's Henry. ... Yes. Of course I'm here. You knew I would be. Were they furious when I didn't turn up at the meeting? ... (*Laughing*) Serve them right. ... (*She listens*) Well, not *quite* what I expected but very pleasant. Charles, dear—all the things in my bedroom are mine, aren't they? I mean probate doesn't apply? ... Oh, good. So would you be so very kind and send some things down. ... The bed and the carpet, and the little chest. And all the curtains. And do you think your Miss Bailey would take my clothes out of the wardrobe and pack them, too? ... No, dear, not the wardrobe—it's too big. But I do want the curtains particularly. And my books. Charles dear, my bits of silver—I'm afraid they'll have to be sold. ... Yes, I know but—oh, thank you. I knew you would. Charles—not the coffee set. I'll keep that. ... (*Pausing*) Well, of course it's special. You gave it to me. ... (*she pauses*) Thank you, my very dear friend. God bless you. Good-night. (*She puts down the phone*)

Voices off R

Dino (*calling*) Henry—we're home!

Dino and Elsie come in R. *Elsie comes* C *to the table. Dino goes to the pegs, takes off his anorak and hangs it up*

Elsie Did Lucy Morris bring the sheets?
Henry She did. And very kindly made up the bed, too. (*Laughing*) Where *did* she get that hat?

Act I

Dino It's her trademark. She wears it in bed. (*He crosses to the fireplace and warms his hands*)

Elsie (*crossing to the window seat*) Right solid old crowd in tonight. (*She sits down and kicks off her shoes*) If I don't get these off, my feet'll drop away from my ankles.

Dino goes to the window seat, kneels down, pulls one of her feet up on to his knee and begins to massage it

You been all right, Miss Henry? Not bored on your own?

Henry Not at all. In fact—(*she pauses*)—Vulcan played up.

Elsie Oh—no!

Henry Not to worry. I've got his measure.

Elsie Good.

She automatically gives Dino's hand a loud slap as it wanders up past her knee

Henry No, apart from that—I certainly haven't been bored.

Dino gets up, yawning and stretching. Elsie pushes her shoes under the valance, gropes for a pair of slippers and puts them on

Dino Henry, old love, would you excuse us if we went to bed? Anything you want, Elsie will——

Henry Not a thing. I'm going up myself in a moment.

Dino crosses and takes her hand

Dino Then—"Good-night, sweet lady. May flights of Botticelli angels lull thee to thy rest."

Henry (*laughing*) "And weave brave dreams about thine idle head."

He kisses her hand and goes to the curtain C, *speaking quietly to Elsie as he passes*

Dino And don't you be long.

He exits C

Elsie gets up goes to the pegs R, *where she takes off her anorak and hangs it up*

Elsie He's always quoting those bits. Half the time, I think he makes them up himself. (*Coming back* C) Miss Henry—I just want to say—I do hope you'll stay a bit—and if you do——

Henry Elsie, I take it it is quite impossible to get Dino to discuss finance?

Elsie He does like to leave that all to me.

Henry (*crisply*) So while I *am* here, I will buy my own food and ask you to accept twenty pounds a week towards expenses. Right . . . ?

Elsie It's more than all right, Miss Henry, and I'll not pretend it isn't. But I do have my pride and—and what Dino and I have got above that—we'll share.

Henry suddenly pulls her into her arms and gives her a tight hug. She lets her go

Elsie runs out C *through the curtain*

Henry goes to the window seat, collects the paintings and puts them behind the curtain L. *She returns to the table, sits down, and pulls the telephone towards her. She dials and waits*

Henry (*On the phone*) Hallo? ... Rupert! ... Yes, Henry ... Wait for it. I'm in Cornwall. ... Yes, absolutely the last outpost of Empire. Have you got a minute? ... Yes, it is. So listen——

Elsie (*off* C) Oh, no, Dino! (*Laughing*) No ... !

A mutter of laughter and some indistinguishable—but apparently enjoyable noises

Henry (*on the phone*) Hold on, will you ...

The noises increase. Henry goes C, *takes off her shoe, reaches up as high as she can, and bangs on the wall. The noises cease. She waits a moment, shoe in hand, then as all is quiet, replaces the shoe and goes to the table, sitting down*

(*On the phone*) Sorry about that ... What? ... Oh, just something I had to attend to. Now listen—I've something very interesting to tell you. ... Interesting—and quite possibly important ...

CURTAIN

ACT II

Scene 1

About a month later. Eleven o'clock on a clear morning

A bright fire burns in the grate. Sun effect outside the windows. The telephone is back on the window sill. A vacuum clearner is heard off C

Mrs Morris enters R *carrying a large carton. She wears a white bibbed apron over a dark dress, and the pansy hat*

Mrs Morris (*calling*) Miss Henry ...! (*She goes to the curtain and calls more loudly*) Miss Henry ...!

The vacuum stops. Henry calls from off C

Henry (*off*) Yes ...?
Mrs Morris Where do you want these books?
Henry (*off*) If you'll start putting them on the dresser, I'll be down in a moment.
Mrs Morris Right you are.

The vacuum restarts. Mrs Morris puts the box down R *of the dresser and begins taking out books and putting them on the main shelf. The vacuum continues for a second then stops*

Henry enters C *through the curtain. She wears a smart flowered overall, and her hair is becomingly tied up in a chiffon scarf. A yellow duster is tucked in the overall pocket*

Henry Mrs Morris, Elsie and I have decided to move the table out of the way—it's really too big ... (*She goes and turns down the other flap of the table*) Would you give me a hand ...
Mrs Morris Where do you want it?
Henry I thought we'd change it with the trolley. Wait a minute—I'll have to pull that out first. (*She goes to the trolley and pulls it across beside the green chair*) And now the table—and the chairs can go each side ...

They push the folded table and the chairs neatly under the pegs

That's better—much more room. We can always pull it out for main meals.

Elsie enters C *through the curtain, carrying a light cleaner, the hose draped over her shoulder. She wears her tweed skirt and a red sweater, and her hair is pinned up out of the way*

Elsie That's about finished, Miss Henry—(*pausing*)—oh, we've moved table, then ...?
Henry Yes. What do you think?
Elsie (*considering*) Yes. Tes much better. And it can always come back again ...
Mrs Morris (*not looking up*) Unless someone decides to nail it to the floor.
Elsie And your room's beautiful—the bed and the little desk—and that lovely Persian rug. Are you going to use all those curtains?
Henry Later, perhaps ... (*She helps Mrs Morris with books*)
Elsie I'll get some of those packing cases into the shed ...

She goes out R *taking the vacuum with her*

Dino comes in from the studio, carrying a bamboo cane about a foot long, and a flower pot containing a small plant some eight inches high. He goes atomatically to the table, starts to put down the pot, realizes, looks round and curses under his breath

Dino Oh, God! (*Calling*) Elsie ... ! (*He goes to the window and puts the plant carefully on the sill. More loudly*) Elsie ... !

Elsie looks in R

Elsie Yes?
Dino Find me a piece of string, will you. About a foot long ...
Elsie You'll have to wait. I'm busy.
Dino I want it now. It's for the tree.
Elsie I'll see what I can do.

She goes back R

Henry Oh, is it today we're planting the tree?
Dino Yes. Merry's bringing up Arthur and Dee. (*He feels in his pockets, gives another mutter of annoyance and goes to the fireplace, feeling along the shelf. He finds a penknife and stands in front of the fire, sharpening the cane*)

Henry crosses L *and pushes up the window. Seagulls are heard. She shakes out her duster and closes the window, then pauses*

Henry Dino, what's this? In this little pot?
Dino *That* is the tree.
Henry But this is only a tiny shoot.
Dino It's growing out of an acorn. (*Crossing*) Careful ... ! Here—see? (*He picks up the pot and indicates carefully with the penknife*) There's the acorn ...
Henry Will it *grow*?
Dino Arthur's going to be very upset if it doesn't.
Henry Why?
Dino He found the acorn and the shoot some months ago and brought it to me. He was worried it might die. So I potted it up and promised in the spring we'd plant it up here. With a proper ceremony.

Act II, Scene 1   23

Henry returns to the dresser

Elsie enters R with a piece of string

Elsie It's all I can find. The length is all right, but you'll have to pick out the knots yourself. (*She goes to the window seat and gives it to him*)

He sits down and tackles the knots with penknife and teeth. A car is heard off L

Here they are!

She pushes up the window. Seagulls are heard, first loud then fainter

Arthur! Dee! Arthur, lovey—say hallo to Elsie! Arthur! Hal-lo . . . !

A child's shrill voice calls, a babble vaguely recognizable as "Hallo"

There's a good boy. (*She shuts the window*) I do wish he'd talk a bit more. Then we might get him to nursery school.

Mrs Morris Some hope . . . ! (*She sweeps all the clutter from the dresser into the now empty carton, leaving only a pile of cups and saucers and glasses*)

Henry (*gently*) Perhaps he's just a late starter.

Merry enters L from the studio. He wears his dog collar, and carries a packet of letters and a separate white envelope

Merry Morning!
Henry ⎫   Good-morning, Merry . . .
Mrs Morris ⎬ (*together*) Morning, Vicar . . .
Dino   ⎪   Hallo, there . . .
Elsie ⎭   Merry dear—I'll get you a coffee . . .

Elsie runs out R

Merry I've brought up the post. (*He puts the packet on the trolley and holds out the white envelope to Henry*) And I met the Admiral on the way up. He asked me to give you this.

Henry For me? I wonder . . . (*She takes her glasses from her overall pocket, puts them on and slits the envelope*)

Merry stands by the fire, warming his hands. Mrs Morris picks up the carton and crosses R

Merry Well, we've got a nice sunny morning for it.
Mrs Morris (*grimly*) It's blowing up a stiffish breeze.

She goes out R

Dino Where's Arthur and Dee?
Merry In the studio. Arthur wanted to take a look at his wall.
Dino (*laughing*) I put in another three cottages yesterday. I wonder if he'll notice . . .

Elsie enters R with a cup of coffee which she takes to Merry

Merry Oh, Elsie darling—thank you. Just what I needed.
Elsie Two sugars . . .

She hurries out R again

Henry (*suddenly*) Oh listen to this. The Admiral's invited me to dine ... (*reading*) "... requests the pleasure—myself and the Reverend Meredith Gane—at the Dower House Monday twenty-third—seven-thirty for eight" ... (*She looks up*) Have you had yours, Merry? Shall you go?
Merry It's obligatory. Once a month I am required to dine with my Churchwarden.
Henry Formal ... ?
Dino Wet suits and decorations essential.
Henry (*turning the letter over*) It does say black tie. What will it be like?
Merry Mrs Morris will cook a superlative meal. Last time the claret was vintage. And afterwards—well, he has an excellent collection of records, and a small but selective library. And the house is tiny, but a gem. Pure Queen Anne.
Henry All this I *cannot* miss.
Merry Do please come. He'll have to behave with courtesy in front of you.
Henry (*taking off her glasses*) Merry, why do you take so much from him?
Merry (*lightly*) He's really very lonely. And my boss insists on tolerance ...
Henry Boss—oh, I see. Well, I'm not too sure about that. (*Grimly*) He who turns other cheek, gets sore face both sides ... (*She puts her glasses in her pocket*)
Merry What's a sore face? They crucified *Him*. (*He drains his cup, puts it on top of the cupboard and glances at his watch*) Dino, do you think we might make a start? I'm standing in for a wedding in Bodmin at three.
Dino (*getting up*) Sure. Come on, everyone. Ceremony now due to begin. (*Calling*) Elsie! Mrs M!

He picks up the pot and cane and goes out L

A child's squeal of delight is heard

Arthur (*off*) Dee-no! Dee-no!
Dino (*off*) Hallo, superman. Up you come, then—on my shoulder. Yes, I've got the tree. (*His voice fades*)

Merry hurries out L after him

Mrs Morris enters R pulling on a cardigan, followed by Elsie

Mrs Morris Tree indeed—up here on a cliff!

She hurries out L. Voices and laughter are heard L dying away

Elsie Miss Henry—are you coming down?
Henry I thought I'd watch from the window. There *are* rather a lot of us, and Arthur might——
Elsie That's a good idea. I'll stay with you ...

She kneels on the window seat below Henry, who remains standing

Henry What exactly is going to happen?
Elsie Dino's got the hole ready. Oh, do look at Arthur—with his little red trowel ...

Act II, Scene 1   25

Henry And then . . . ?
Elsie Dino plants the tree. With Arthur helping. And Merry gives a blessing. And then Dino says the tree prayer. It's a poem.
Henry I don't remember anything like that in the poems you showed me.
Elsie He only made it up last night. Just rattled it off—oh, there we go . . .

She pushes up the window. Voices are heard off, and seagulls

> He's put the tree in. Look at Arthur patting away with his trowel. Now Merry's giving the blessing——

Voices and gulls die away. Merry's voice is heard indistinguishable in the distance

> —and now Dino'll say the prayer.

Henry We should have gone down. We can't hear it up here . . .
Elsie (*quietly, looking out of the window*)
        Lord, bless this tree
        And make it grow
        Until it reach the sky
        And grant, O Lord,
        That I may know
        Its joy before I die.

She looks at Henry

> What's the matter, Miss Henry? Isn't it a good poem?

Henry (*gently*) It isn't a poem, Elsie. It's a delightful little jingle for a child. And something Dino's very good at——

Suddenly a child's shrill screaming and a confusion of voices off L

Mrs Morris ⎫		Arthur—Arthur—NO!
Merry ⎬	(*off together*)	Dino—look out . . .
Dino ⎭		Arthur—stop—stop it . . .

The sounds become louder

Elsie What's happening? Oh—Arthur's hitting Dino with the trowel—he's in one of his tempers—(*calling*)—Arthur—no! Oh, no—he's starting to run!

The confusion increases

Mrs Morris ⎫		Watch him—watch him—don't let him run . . .
Merry ⎬	(*off together*)	Catch him—Arthur—come back. . .
Dino ⎭		Arthur—come here—someone head him off

A woman's hysterical scream rises above everything

Delia (*off*) HE'S GOING OVER THE CLIFF . . . !
Elsie Oh, my God . . . !

She runs L. *Henry pulls her back*

Henry No—stay here. There's plenty of them. They'll cope. Look, Merry's got Arthur. It's all right . . .

Delia's screams increase

Elsie Now he's set Dee off. Once she get's started—I must go——
Henry No, Elsie—no! (*Leaning out of the window*) Merry! Dino! Bring Delia up here. Bring her up HERE! (*To Elsie*) Go and make a cup of coffee. Black and strong. Quickly . . .

Elsie runs off R

Henry moves the trolley in front of the fire and pulls the green armchair out beside it, shaking up the cushion

The screaming comes nearer. Merry and Dino enter L, *half-carrying, half-supporting Delia between them*

Delia is a plain scrawny girl of about twenty-three. She wears a flowered dress, an ugly plain cardigan and wrinkled tights. Her short hair is sticking up on end, her face is blotched and contorted. She continues to scream, though not so loudly

Here . . .

She helps them get Delia into the chair, where she struggles, trying to fight them off

Dino Now, stop it, Dee—stop it—d'you hear!

Henry goes to the dresser

Merry Delia—everything is all *right*!
Delia He went over the cliff!

Dino goes behind the chair and holds her firmly by the shoulders

Merry He did NOT go over the cliff. Mrs Morris has got him. He's all right.
Delia—Arthur's all *right*!

Henry has poured a small glass of brandy. She comes to Delia's left

Delia . . . !

Delia's screams die to sobbing. Suddenly she throws her arms over her head and rocks herself to and fro. Henry offers the glass

Henry Delia—drink this . . .

Delia continues to sob and rock

Merry Come along, now. Drink this.

He takes the glass from Henry. Henry pulls Delia's arms down. Merry almost forces the brandy down her throat. She gasps, splutters and is quiet

Dino (*cheerfully*) She'll live. I'll get back to Arthur.

He pats Delia on the back and hurries out L

Merry straightens up and puts the glass on the trolley

Merry She'll calm down now. You can cope, can't you?

Act II, Scene 1   27

> *He runs out* L
>
> *Elsie enters* R, *carrying a tray with four mugs and the coffee filter. She puts the tray on the trolley and fills a mug*

Elsie Miss Henry—I'm that sorry ...
Henry (*taking the mug*) It's all right, Elsie. Leave it to me. Go and tell them to cope with Arthur in the studio. If we bring him in here, she may start off again.
Elsie Yes, Miss Henry.

> *She runs off* L

Delia (*suddenly yelling*) Wah-wah-wah!
Henry That will do! Now—take a deep breath——
Delia Wah-wah-wah!
Henry A deep breath!

> *Delia opens her mouth for another wail. Henry raises a warning finger*

Delia—NO!

> *Delia looks at her. Then closes her mouth and is quiet*

(*Severely*) I should *think* so. Now—deep breath. Come along—that's right. And another. And again. Fine. Now drink this.

> *She holds the mug to Delia's lips. Delia sips once, then again, then grabs the mug in both hands, drains it and gives it back to Henry*

Good girl. (*She puts the mug on the trolley, takes a handkerchief from her pocket and wipes Delia's lips*) Now, let's get it absolutely clear. Arthur did NOT go over the cliff.
Delia (*wildly*) I wish he had! I WISH HE HAD!
Henry Delia——!
Delia I don't want him! I don't like him! I never h-a-v-e! (*Her voice rises to a wail. She puts her arms over her head and starts rocking and sobbing again*)
Henry Just sit quiet a moment. (*She kneels by the chair and puts a comforting arm round Delia's shoulder*)
Delia I'm wicked! I'm wicked! (*She buries her face on Henry's shoulder*)
Henry (*quietly*) No, you're not. Quiet, now, there ...

> *She holds Delia against her. Delia's sobs quieten*
>
> *Mrs Morris enters* L

Mrs Morris We'll have to clean him up in the studio. Bathroom's too small. Is she ... ?
Henry She's going to be all right. (*Quietly*) How's Arthur?
Mrs Morris (*tartly*) Apart from wetting himself like a firehose and then rolling in all the mud available, he's all right too. I need hot water ...

> *She goes out* R
>
> *Delia moves away from Henry and sits back in the chair. She makes a childish*

groping movement towards Henry's pocket. Henry takes out her handkerchief and gives it to her. She mops her face. Suddenly she begins to talk

Delia I thought—a little baby. Sort of—pretty. And warm. I thought it would be—nice.
Henry But Delia——
Delia Arthur isn't nice. He makes puddles. And messes. And he screams. And smells.
Henry If you really feel———
Delia (*not listening*) Once he made a puddle in the shop. And it was FULL! (*Her voice rises on the last word*)
Henry Delia——
Delia Behind the fridge. And it all spread out. Two sacks of new potatoes ruined. (*Her voice rising again*) Why couldn't he have gone the other end—by the BAKED BEANS!

Abruptly Henry gets up and crosses to the window. In spite of everything, she cannot quite stifle laughter. Delia continues to sob and scrub her face

And the Admiral was there. He *roared*. He said the place was awash.

Henry turns. She has regained her composure

Henry (*comfortingly*) I'm sure it wasn't up to flood level. And you soon got it cleared up.
Delia (*abruptly*) The Admiral cleared it up.
Henry The Admiral——?
Delia He fetched Willy over. And they took down a big can of disinfectant and cleaned everything and then they moved the fridge against the wall and fixed it so that Arthur couldn't get behind again. (*She pauses for breath*)

Mrs Morris enters R carrying a large plastic bowl and with two large towels over her shoulder. She marches straight across and goes out L without speaking

And then the Admiral paid for the disinfectant. I saw him put it in the till.
Henry I think in the circumstances he was very helpful.
Delia I hate him. He *roars* at me. And when he comes in the shop now he sniffs and pokes about. (*Suddenly*) It makes me want to hit him. (*Viciously*) One day, I will.
Henry Delia, about Arthur——
Delia I hate him, too. I can't cope.
Henry Have you ever thought of putting him into care?
Delia Oh, I couldn't do that, Miss Henry. Because of his dad.
Henry (*quietly*) Delia—who *was* his father?
Delia I don't know.
Henry But surely——
Delia He came into the shop one lunchtime. We were closed but he tapped on the window and I let him in. (*Slowly*) He was—nice.
Henry (*gently*) Yes?

Act II, Scene 1   29

Delia All smiling. And—fun. He had some samples. Spirits. Little coloured bottles in a case. And he made me feel—nice.
Henry What happened?
Delia (*simply*) We went behind the fridge.

Henry involuntarily puts a hand over her face for a second

(*Looking back into the past*) It was—nice.
Henry You never saw him again?
Delia No. I just got Arthur. So you do see, Miss Henry, I couldn't put him away. His dad wouldn't want me to do that. (*Suddenly she yawns hugely, stretches, curls herself up in the chair and is instantly asleep*)
Henry (*shaking her gently*) Dee—Dee . . . (*She looks at her for a moment. Suddenly she takes off her chiffon scarf, smooths down the spiky hair and ties the scarf neatly over Delia's head*)

Dino and Merry enter L. *Merry carries his jacket over his shoulder, and his shirt-sleeves are rolled above his elbows*

Dino (*cheerfully*) We've got it all organized. At least Merry has . . . (*He pauses, looking at Delia*) Well, look at this then!
Henry Exhaustion.
Merry Physical and mental. (*He drops his jacket on the brown armchair and rolls down his sleeves*) Mrs Morris is taking them both home. She's going to put them both straight to bed and get Doc Prentis to come and give them a sedative. She says they can stay there for a few days until they settle down again. (*He puts on his jacket*) Then it looks as though we shall have to do something with the Social Services . . .
Dino It looks as though we shall have to close the shop.
Henry But that's their livelihood . . .
Dino Let's hope it will only be temporary.
Henry Dino, why don't I go down there and carry on for——
Dino You, old Henry? Don't be ridiculous. You'd never manage a shop.
Henry (*rather tartly*) If I could cope with a selfish restless old egotist for nearly thirty years, I can certainly manage a village shop for a couple of weeks.
Merry I think it might be a very good idea. We'll talk about it later. (*He looks at Delia*) Dino, I think we can get her down into the car without waking her.
Dino Sure.
Henry I always feel uneasy about that weak handrail. Are you ever going to fix it because we could ask——
Dino (*laughing*) I'll do it quietly tomorrow. (*Bending over Delia*) Come you away, my 'andsome. Yo ho and up she rises!

Merry helps him get Delia across his shoulder in a fireman's lift, and goes to pull aside the studio curtain

Dino carries Delia out L

Merry turns

See you all on Sunday. Don't forget.

He goes out L

Henry crosses to the window and looks out. Voices are heard off L

Elsie	⎫	Oh, do be careful ...
Dino	⎪	It's all right if we keep over to the left.
Arthur	⎬ (*off, together*)	Dee-no. Want Dee-no ...
Mrs Morris	⎪	Now Arthur—you behave ...
Merry	⎭	Take it easy round this bit ...

Henry moves the trolley back beside the green chair. She puts a log on fire (fireglow up) and plugs in the kettle. A car drives off in the distance

Elsie comes in L

Elsie Oh, Miss Henry, what must you think of us.
Henry I think everyone has behaved admirably. Come and sit down. You look worn out.

Elsie sits in the armchair L

Elsie Why *does* Dee have to go off like that?
Henry She lives under great stress.
Elsie Yes, I know we ought to do something about her and Arthur. I just don't know what.

Dino comes in L *whistling. He carries a sketch-pad and pencil*

Dino All nice and tidied up. Except the studio. That rug'll never be the same. Anyone making coffee? (*He sits on the window seat and begins to sketch*)

Elsie automatically gets up, as the kettle boils

Henry Stay where you are.

During the next sequence, Henry refills the filter and pours three mugs of coffee

You know, I've been thinking about the Admiral's invitation. It's a little awkward. I shall have to return hospitality. I suppose—one could go to a hotel ...
Dino (*laughing*) Give 'em dinner here.
Henry Here ... ?
Dino Why not? Mrs Morris'll cook for you and Elsie'll get you something off the wine. You can clean the room up a bit. Or not. Do the Master Mariner good to go slumming. Go on—I dare you!
Henry Dino, would you mind ... ?

Elsie crosses to him with two mugs and gives him one

Dino Not so long as I don't have to come. (*Taking coffee*) Thanks, love.
Henry I'll certainly think about it.

Act II, Scene 1

She takes out her glasses from her pocket, puts them on and opens her letter. Elsie looks at Dino's sketch

Elsie Let me see—(*pausing*)—it's ...
Dino (*laughing*) Portrait of sleeping girl.
Elsie It *is* Dee. (*Slowly*) Did you have to make her look such a mess ...

Henry glances up from her letter

Henry (*gently*) One day we'll go into Plymouth and see what a really good hairdresser can do.

Elsie returns to the armchair L, and drinks her coffee. Dino continues sketching

Dino What did Merry mean by saying see you all on Sunday?
Henry (*intent on her letter*) We're all going to morning service.
Dino All ... ? (*He drinks his coffee and puts the mug on the floor*)
Henry It's time we started to build him a congregation. Mrs M. is picking up Delia. And the Bennetts are coming—thank goodness. There are seven of them. Have you got a suit?
Dino Of course, I've got a suit. I don't need it to——
Henry You need to look neat when you read the lesson.
Dino Henry! If you've said I'll——
Henry I only said I'd ask you, dear. But Merry was so pleased. You can't disappoint him. It's your educated voice——
Dino Henry, you had no right to make arrangements for me without——
Henry (*calmly*) You'll do it beautifully, dear. And it's that really dramatic bit about Uriah the Hittite being put in the forefront of the battle.
Dino If I——
Henry Oh by the way, there's a letter for you.

She picks up a letter from the trolley and throws it over. He catches it

Dino Oh it's nothing—some circular or other.
Henry I think I should open it if I were you. You never know—it might be some special offer.

Dino slits the envelope and takes out the letter

(*To Elsie*) I'm still not sure about my little dinner party. I suppose there isn't a private room at *The Lobster*?
Elsie Not really. There's a little bit of a place at the back, but it——
Dino (*suddenly*) Henry! What the devil have you been up to ... ! (*He jumps up, holding the letter. He is now really angry*)
Henry (*quietly*) I really don't know what you mean——
Dino I bet you damn well do! (*Reading*) "We have examined with considerable interest the colour photographs recently sent to us regarding your work. Also the poems and sketches for the juvenile market. We should like to discuss the possibility of your writing and illustrating a children's book——"
Elsie Oh, Dino!
Dino (*reading*) "We cannot, of course, commission at this stage, but perhaps you could call and talk to us at our London Office. Or if you

wish, one of our Directors, Rupert Dominic, would be prepared to come down and visit——" (*Disgustedly*) Some cheapskate set-up—Dominic Publications——
Henry I know, dear. I've had one too. (*She picks up her letter and reads*) "Dear Henry, The paintings show much promise, the poems are charming and we are all intrigued by the Wall. Do you think he would discuss it with us? Eric is impressed, definitely. Love . . ." and there's a PS. "This is a very clever boy." (*She puts down the letter and takes off her glasses*) Eric is the Chairman. And a very knowledgeable man——
Dino You actually sneaked into the studio and took photos—colour photos—of——
Henry I only have a small camera now, but it *is* first class. Fabian always insisted that where photography was concerned, we had the best.
Dino And the poems! Elsie, how dare you——
Elsie (*distressed*) Oh, Dino!
Henry Elsie only showed me the poems because she is so proud of them.
Dino You poked and pried about—and never even asked my permission——
Henry Would you have given it?
Dino The hell I would!
Henry So I took a chance (*She puts the letter in her pocket*) You don't have to do anything, of course. It just seems a pity to waste even a small talent. And Dominic's are a very well-established and forward-looking company. They published Fabian's books.
Dino Fabian wrote extremely dull and pedantic volumes on a highly specialized subject.
Henry In their own field, they made a lot of money.
Dino Money! Don't keep on about money! I don't need it. I'm living the kind of life I want. Peaceful. Free. To hell with the rat race. And that's my last word.
Henry Dino, why——
Dino You got those photographs in a very underhand way. And I don't like the sound of this—this Rupert person. He—gushes. Listen—I've got a PS too. (*Reading*) "Your ideas are very original. Such a nice change from pussies and bunnies." (*Looking up*) Pussies and bunnies! Yuk!
Henry Oh, that's just a camp act. Rupert is a very shrewd young entrepreneur.
Dino Then let him stick to his pusssies and bunnies and leave me alone!
Henry Dino, I used to do all Fabian's preparation and manuscripts. I could help. The book—would it really be so much work——
Dino Work! There you go again! You and Elsie. You're obsessed with it—like a couple of frenzied juggernauts. It's all I hear these days—work!
Elsie Dino!
Dino Work! Work! A horrible Greek chorus. Woe! Woe! Woe!
Henry I'm sorry—(*she pauses, speaking to herself*)—a Greek chorus . . . (*Quietly*) Very well dear. I'm sorry if you thought I was interfering.
Dino I know you meant well. But that's enough, both of you. It is not to be mentioned again. Understand? (*He tears the letter in half, throws it down, picks up his pad and pencil, goes* L, *and turns*) And that table goes back where it's always been. Today.

Act II, Scene 1   33

He goes off into the studio

A pause

Henry (*to herself*) Oh, dear ...
Elsie (*quietly*) You'll not move him now Miss Henry. I know this mood.
Henry I thought it worth a try.
Elsie Like he says—it's his way, isn't it? Leave him alone and he's contented—and good-tempered—and fun. And he doesn't need much. To paint when he feels like it—a bottle of wine. He just doesn't want to work.
Henry Nor do lots of people. But they have to just the same.
Elsie He doesn't have to. He's got his benefit.
Henry Benefit? Oh, yes.
Elsie He gives it to me, and I give him some back, and we get along all right in our way. Sometimes—sometimes I think—but there it is. If he were to be changed maybe we wouldn't be—as we are. (*Pausing*) Miss Henry, may I tell you something? Something private?
Henry Only if you won't regret it later.
Elsie No, I'd like to tell someone. I can't tell Dino. It would spoil things.
Henry How?
Elsie If you'll just pull open that dresser drawer—the left—a little box—right at the back.

Henry does so, bringing out a small oblong box

Henry This?
Elsie That's right. Open it.

Henry brings out a star-shaped locket on a gold chain

Dino gave it to me. It's a star—see?
Henry A star—(*remembering*)—yes. It's lovely, Elsie. Here—put it on. (*She puts the chain over Elsie's head*)
Elsie He saw it in a paper and bought it. He was so pleased. And so was I.
Henry But of course you were ...
Elsie Well, when I went to put it back in the box—it was mail order, see?—I found the bill. (*Pausing*) Miss Henry, it cost thirty pounds.
Henry Does it matter. I don't suppose he buys you something every week——
Elsie Miss Henry, where would he get thirty pounds?
Henry The sketches for visitors——
Elsie In the winter? When we're deserted? No, it right worried me. And then I remembered. Two weeks before, I'd given him the money to pay the electric.
Henry (*quietly*) Oh.
Elsie I found the receipt. All screwed up in the pocket of his jeans.
Henry He *had* paid it——
Elsie He'd paid half.
Henry I see. Well, I don't want to pry into your affairs—whatever Dino may say—but is this really——
Elsie We manage quite all right if the bills don't run behind. Once we got in a muddle—but you do see I couldn't say anything?

Henry Yes. But he *is* irresponsible.
Elsie He's happy and loving. (*She looks defiantly at Henry*) And he's a right fine man in bed.
Henry (*quietly*) So what happened—about the electric?
Elsie I did two weeks' double-time, and now I pay all the bills myself. (*Slowly*) Miss Henry, why do people always tell you things? Merry says the same.
Henry (*quietly*) Perhaps my uncle taught me to be a good listener.
Elsie Well, as I said, you won't move him now.
Henry (*abruptly*) Elsie, do you read much?
Elsie (*surprised*) When I get the time. Library van comes every second Tuesday. Don't look so surprised. I suppose Dino told you I was gormless.
Henry Well——
Elsie I got three A levels. One for English Lit. Why did you ask?
Henry I wondered if you'd be interested in a book I found this morning when I was unpacking.
Elsie What's it called?
Henry *Lysistrata*. It's a girl's name.
Elsie (*laughing*) I bet that got a giggle at her christening.
Henry I doubt if she *was* christened. She lived in Greece about two thousand years ago.
Elsie What did she do to get written about?
Henry She stopped a war.
Elsie All by herself? How?
Henry She rallied all the women of the city. Until their men stopped fighting, they were refused all favours.
Elsie All favours? (*Pausing*) Oh, I see. (*Laughing*) Got desperate, did they—the men?
Henry Extremely.
Elsie Tes natural enough.
Henry And a very simple way to stop something. (*Slowly*) Or to get something started.
Elsie Oh yes, I can see it would—(*she pauses*)—it would work both ways.
Henry Providing everyone is *very* firm.
Elsie (*thoughtfully*) Yes, indeed. And it would have to be worth it.
Henry That, too. (*Getting up*) Dear me, how time does go when one is talking trivialities. I must go and finish my room.
Elsie Miss Henry, might I borrow that book?
Henry Certainly. (*She goes to the dresser and looks along books*) Actually, it's a play—ah, here we are—(*she pulls out a small green book*)—and it's in blank verse. But the story is very clearly set out in the preface, and the translation is excellent.
Elsie Oh. I see.
Henry You might enjoy it.

She puts the book on the trolley and goes off C *through the curtain*

Elsie looks down at the book, then across at the torn letter, goes and picks it up. *She fits the torn halves together, reads it, then folds it up and puts it in her pocket. She picks up the book and starts to open it*

Dino comes in L *whistling. He has now recovered his good humour*

Elsie hastily puts the book down

Dino Have we got any turps? Arthur's trodden chrome yellow all over the rug . . .
Elsie You left it in the kitchen yesterday . . .
Dino Oh, yes. Bring it in to me, will you, there's a love . . .

He turns L. *Elsie comes down to him*

Elsie Dino—just a minute . . .
Dino (*turning*) Yes . . . ?
Elsie Won't you really do anything about—about that book?
Dino Now don't you start . . .
Elsie You could think about it.
Dino I'm not going to waste time thinking about something which isn't going to materialize.
Elsie Miss Henry says it might make some money.
Dino Look, love, Henry's been used to money all her life. Now she's got to get used to doing without it. We do, and we're all right.
Elsie It would be nice to have just a little more. Enough to keep the bills going without worrying.
Dino We don't owe anything now, do we?
Elsie No.
Dino Then why talk about worrying? Find me the turps, will you—and a cloth . . . (*He crosses* L *to the studio*)
Elsie Dino——

He turns

—if you just did this one book. And perhaps——
Dino Now, look here——
Elsie —perhaps we could get rid of Vulcan—and get a new car—and that handrail did ought to be mended——
Dino Vulcan is indestructible, the car has just had a new battery. And as for the handrail——
Elsie Dino——
Dino I'll do it quietly tomorrow. (*He tweaks her nose and gives her a quick kiss*) So stop bothering your little head about nothing. (*Pausing, quietly*) You're wearing your star. (*He lifts the locket*) Still like it?
Elsie (*quietly*) Yes.
Dino Good. Because it's the nearest I'll ever get to giving you the Crown Jewels.
Elsie I don't want the Crown Jewels.
Dino I should hope not. Great top heavy over-stuffed things. And the only real jewel for you, my innocent, is a daisy chain.

He kisses her lightly again and goes out L *to the studio*

Elsie stands looking after him for a moment, then she sighs. She becomes very busy, collecting all the mugs and Merry's cup and saucer on to the tray on the trolley

> *Elsie picks up the tray, knocking the green book on to the floor, and goes out R. A pause — then she comes running back R, looking round the trolley. She sees the book, picks it up, pauses, then looks through the pages for a second. Then she looks across L to the studio*

Elsie (*quietly*) Daisy chain . . . !

She shuts the book with a snap, tightens her lips and goes out R

CURTAIN

SCENE 2

About five weeks later. Morning

The room is unchanged

Dino (*off* L) Elsie . . . !

He comes in from the studio

Elsie . . . !

Elsie comes down C through the curtain. She wears the same sweater and jeans and carries a small suitcase

Oh, there you are. Make us some coffee, will you?
Elsie You'll have to make it yourself. I haven't time.

She crosses R. Dino intercepts her

Dino Elsie, love — what's the matter?
Elsie There's nothing the matter.
Dino There damn well is. You're never here more than a couple of nights a week, and when you are — (*pausing*) — you just keep saying "no". Why?
Elsie Does there have to be a reason?
Dino After all those noes there ruddy well does. (*Suddenly he takes the case, puts it on the floor and pulls her round to face him*) Elsie — you're not pregnant?
Elsie (*pulling away*) If I'm not, it's no thanks to you.
Dino That's all right, then. (*Putting his arms round her*) Come on, love. It's — it's been over a month——
Elsie (*pulling away again*) Oh, let me alone can't you! Go and get on with your work.
Dino What work?
Elsie Get started on that book.
Dino I don't want to do *that* book. I have no intention of even thinking about *that* book.
Elsie Then I've no intention about the other thing.

Act II, Scene 2

Dino (*blankly*) I don't believe it. You actually mean that's what this is all about?
Elsie Yes.
Dino It's nothing more nor less than emotional blackmail!
Elsie Whatever it is, I'm still saying "no".
Dino (*suddenly*) Elsie—has Henry put you up to this?
Elsie Miss *Henry*? That's a right *disgraceful* thing to suggest!
Dino *Has* she?
Elsie (*indignant*) If you think I'd be so—so *indecent*—as to talk about what we do in bed——
Dino Elsie——!
Elsie —and to an old maiden like Miss Henry—you should be downright ashamed of yourself!

They have now both lost their tempers

Dino All right! All *right!* I apologize. But I still want to know why you're behaving like this.
Elsie And I want you to write that book and make us some money.
Dino Money...! We're all right as we are.
Elsie You may be. I've tried to explain to you but you won't listen. I don't want you to be a millionaire——
Dino Oh, *thank* you!
Elsie But I'm tired of scratting and scrapping up tenpenny pieces. So I've thought it all out. (*Pausing, then deliberately*) No book. No bed.
Dino (*laughing ironically*) And have you thought what you'll be missing?
Elsie Who says I'll be missing anything? There's a big sea outside, Dino Ellis. And plenty of fish in it!
Dino Elsie—you wouldn't——
Elsie I wouldn't need to do more than crook my finger and have them lining up to nibble it. With Willy Flagg ahead of the queue!
Dino How dare you mention Willy Flagg? He has hair in his ears!
Elsie His ears don't notice in bed. And in a good season that garage can make just about two hundred pounds a week!
Dino All this fuss about a miserable two hundred pounds——
Elsie So I'll make a bargain with you. I'm moving in with Dee. And you can do your book on ration.
Dino What——!
Elsie Three pages of writing and two drawings. Then you can ring me. And I'll come back——
Dino You'd *better!*
Elsie —for one night. Then you'll do some more and I'll come back again. Till it's finished. Then we'll think what you're going to do next.
Dino And suppose I do nothing!
Elsie Then nothing is what you'll get.
Dino Oh, is it! There are *female* fish in that big sea!
Elsie No use trawling your net in the village, Dino Ellis! I've put the word round that you're on the hunt. (*She picks up her suitcase and crosses* R)
Dino Elsie——!

Elsie turns at the door R

Elsie And if you go into the town, you'll find you have to pay for it!

She runs out R. *The door slams*

Dino Elsie——! (*He runs to the window and pushes it up*) ELSIE——!

A seagull gives a raucous cry "Wak-wak-wak" like mocking laughter

Shut up, you blasted bird! It isn't funny! (*He slams down the window, and paces across the room. Suddenly*) I will not—I will NOT—be pressurized. (*Calling*) Henry! Henry! Where are you?
Henry (*off* C) Just coming, dear.

She enters C *through the curtain, wearing a coat, and carrying her handbag and a small case*

Do you want me?
Dino What do you mean by interfering in my sex life?
Henry (*shocked*) Dino——!
Dino Oh, come off it! Elsie wouldn't have thought this up by herself.
Henry Whatever Elsie may have thought up, I'm sure it is very right and reasonable.
Dino Right! Reasonable!

Henry becomes very quiet and dignified

Henry I am of course very grateful that you have invited me here, but if you feel I have—however unwittingly—caused any trouble—or embarrassment—I am quite prepared to leave.
Dino I will NOT be made to feel guilty!
Henry As it happens, I shall not be here for the next few days, so if you want to think things over——
Dino Where're you going?
Henry I'm staying with Delia till Wednesday. We're all going to paint out the shop.
Dino Why wasn't I asked?
Henry Elsie thought perhaps not. We do have Merry helping, and in the evenings Willy Flagg.
Dino (*through his teeth*) This is a plot. A concerted diabolical plot.
Henry I haven't the least idea what you're talking about. You'll manage I'm sure. And if you don't want to cook, you can always come down to *The Lobster*.
Dino I shall stay here and die of starvation!
Henry (*calmly*) Not in four days, dear, surely? The fridge is stocked up. Milk and bread. And lots of tins. Soup and fruit. And plenty of baked beans. (*She crosses* R)
Dino I hate baked beans!
Henry Oh, I don't know, dear—with curry sauce and oven-ready chips, you might find them quite acceptable.

She goes out R

Act II, Scene 2

Dino Hell and damnation! (*He paces the room, kicks the window seat, and suddenly picks up the phone from the sill and dials. On the phone*) Dino here. Put Elsie on. ... Yes ... (*He waits fidgetting with the cord*) Yes? ... Yes? (*Listening*) What? Making sandwiches for Willy Flagg! Thank *you*. (*He slams down the phone, looks round the room and suddenly snaps his fingers*) Right ... ! (*He goes into furious action, pulls the table* C, *puts up one flap as usual, runs the trolley down below the door. He returns* C *and looks round triumphantly*) Right ... !

The phone rings. He snatches it up

Elsie ... ? ... Oh, hallo, Sab. ... How's your love life? ... Mine. ... Brilliant. ... Yes—not at the moment. Sab, for God's sake—why does everyone keep saying "So what do we do about Henry?" Don't any of you realize what Henry is doing to everyone else! ... Right. Bye. ... Oh, Sab—I saw some of your ads, for "Grip-U-Girdles". Put your layout man against the wall of the studio and send out for a machine gun. (*He slams down the phone, turns restlessly up* C, *takes up the kettle, shakes it, finds it empty and curses under his breath. He returns to the window and gazes moodily out. Then he turns down* L *to the studio—and stops*) No—I'm damned if I will!

Rupert Dominic enters R. *She is a very smart young woman in her thirties— wearing a light summer suit and silk shirt. Her hair is fashionably set and she wears expensive costume jewellery—gold necklet, bracelets, rings, and a pair of horn-rimmed glasses on a gold safety chain. She carries an efficient portable typewriter in a cream leather case, has a matching cream briefcase, and under a laid-back manner is a very formidable young executive*

Rupert Hallo. You must be Dino. (*She puts the typewriter on the trolley*) Do you always leave your front door so conveniently open?
Dino Who the hell are you?
Rupert Rupert Dominic.
Dino Rupert—I thought——
Rupert So *tiresome* explaining ... (*She comes* C *to the table and puts down her briefcase*) My parents desperately wanted a boy. To be called Rupert. When I turned up, they christened me Ruperta. I ask you—how could anyone possibly live with a name like that?
Dino I ought to break your neck.
Rupert (*lightly*) Deary me—what *have* these poor bones done?
Dino Why did you start all this nonsense about an idiot book?
Rupert I think you might do a very good children's book. I keep writing and telling you, but you never answer ...
Dino So ... ?
Rupert So I've come down to see you about it.
Dino All the way from London? In a helicopter, I presume?
Rupert A Porsche, actually. I'm staying in Plymouth.
Dino This, of course, has all been most carefully arranged by Henry.
Rupert Henry ... ? (*Raising her right hand*) I do solemnly swear by whoever

or whatever, that Henry does not—repeat NOT—know I am here at this moment.

Dino And Henry has told you nothing about anything else?

Rupert What is there to tell? (*Glancing at her wrist-watch*) I thought we might work a bit this afternoon and evening, and perhaps fit in a little time tomorrrow——

Dino Oh, *did* you!

Rupert —but I positively must be back in town on Monday. It's just on twelve. Why don't we do a couple of hours and then break for lunch?

Dino There's no food in the house.

Rupert I brought it with me. Would you like to go down and fetch it up?

Dino Now, look——

Rupert Big green Harrods' box. Just a few bits and pieces. Paté and ham—rolls and fruit. And one of their special casseroles. All we do is heat it up.

Dino All you do is take it back again——

Rupert Tenderest morsels of fillet steak in red wine, with a breath—the merest breath, I promise you—of garlic——

Dino I said——

Rupert —and served with tiny tiny mushrooms in a cream sauce. (*She opens her briefcase and takes out a large packet of photographs*) Where's Henry? And Elsie?

Dino Henry is staying down in the village. Painting out a shop.

Rupert That doesn't surprise me. And Elsie?

Dino Elsie has ft home and will not return.

Rupert looks up from the photos

Rupert Not return . . . ?

Dino Until I agree to produce a certain specified amount of work within a certain specified time.

Rupert And shall you? Agree?

Dino Never. And I still don't believe you and Henry don't know all about it.

Rupert (*raising her hand*) I do solemnly swear——

Dino All right, all right. You know now. So you and Harrods can get back in the car and laugh your bloody heads off all up the M-Four.

Rupert On the contrary. I've not yet met the original, but having seen the photograph, I can assure you of my deepest sympathies.

Dino Let me see those . . . (*He crosses and takes the photos*)

Rupert We enlarged them, of course. Henry did a good job. (*She watches him look at the photos*) How long has this—er—deprivation—been going on?

Dino Three weeks and four days.

Rupert Good God . . . ! Something must be done immediately.

Dino Just *go*.

Rupert We'll do some work—rough out the book, perhaps, and then we'll have lunch. You'll feel better after some good food. (*She takes a bunch of keys from her briefcase*)

Dino Do you never give up?

Act II, Scene 2   41

Rupert In the boot. Keys.

She throws them over. He catches them

Be careful with that box up the path. There's four bottles of wine in it.

They look at each other for a moment. Dino puts the photos down on the table

Dino I'll eat your damned casserole. I'm not doing any book.
Rupert Of course not. I've merely come down to cook your lunch.

He mutters under his breath and goes out R

Rupert puts on her glasses. She takes a small note-book from her briefcase and checks something. Then she crosses to the telephone and dials

Hallo? ... Is that the shop—the Stores? ... Is Miss Ellis there? ... Yes, urgent.... I'll hold.... (*Pause*) Henry! ... Yes, about twenty minutes ... Perfect timing—he's still reeling from the blow ... What? Well, I can be tough too. I've driven three hundred miles and ever since I arrived I've been lying my head off—on oath. If I'm to undertake long-term perjury, I want an end product. Now listen. When you come back, be absolutely normal. Notice nothing and say less. Ring me Tuesday night.... About eleven. Call box. Transfer charge.... Yes, I will reveal every sordid detail. Whatever happens, don't let Elsie come back. And by the way, I hope you've got that damned book hidden. If he ever finds it, we're finished. (*Pausing*) Yes.... That's clear, then.... What? ... Elsie is ... ? Buy her a bottle of gin and a chastity belt. (*She puts down the phone just as* ...)

Dino enters R *lugging the green Harrods' box*

Dino Who was that?
Rupert Wrong number. Some woman going on and on about a dogs' home. Take that into the kitchen, will you? The white wine can go in the fridge. Leave one bottle of red out for lunch. And the casserole should go in the oven at slow.

Dino mutters under his breath and goes out R

Rupert fetches the typewriter from the trolley, takes it out of the case on the table, puts the case on the floor. She opens her briefcase, takes out papers etc., organizing everything neatly. Then she fetches a chair from up L *and puts it* R *of the table. She goes across* L, *pulls aside the studio curtain and looks in*

Rupert goes in. Pause. A small crash

(*Off*) Good God ... !

She returns L, *coughing, and brushes off her hands, goes to the table, finds a handkerchief in her briefcase, fastidiously dusts down her suit, takes off her glasses and polishes them*

Dino enters R

Sit down. No—sit *down*. Use your energy for your brain, not to prop up your legs.

She puts on her glasses. Dino sits on the window seat

Now—as I keep saying—we'll rough out the book, and after lunch—with your permission—I'll have a look through the studio.
Dino And what do you think you're likely to find?
Rupert I know exactly what I'm going to find. The usual predictable rubbish—Elsie and the Master Mariner—(*looking through the photos*)—first class. And hopefully plenty of pleasant saleable stuff. Enough for a small exhibition.
Dino Ex——
Rupert We'll time it with publication day. A striking display on antique tables—Georgian, I think—nice and solid—against the background of Arthur's wall——
Dino Are you proposing to hold this exhibition here—in the studio . . . ?
Rupert Don't be ridiculous. I've applied for the Braganza.
Dino Braganza . . . ?
Rupert Braganza. Elegant little gallery just off Bond Street. Small, but intimate. Just right for a first showing.
Dino What about the Wall? Am I supposed to reproduce that damned scribble——
Rupert Certainly not. We'll photograph it in sections and set it up on the spot.
Dino I've told you——
Rupert Come and look at the plan.

She takes a drawing from her briefcase and flattens it out on the table. Dino goes slowly over

Long and narrow, see? This end—the Wall with tables. Pictures down both sides. This end—(*indicating with a pencil*)—has two long windows—there. We'll hang the space between with velvet—crimson, probably——
Dino Crimson velvet! That's a cliché, if you like.
Rupert I do so agree, but it always lights well. And here—right in the centre of everything—the statement.
Dino Statement . . . ?
Rupert The dominating picture. "Morning Star".
Dino (*quietly*) No.
Rupert Very careful soft lighting——
Dino (*crossing to the window seat*) I said no.
Rupert Dino——
Dino No.
Rupert Why not?
Dino Because nobody looks at Elsie in the nude but me.
Rupert (*coolly deliberate*) And that's a bit problematical at the moment, isn't it?
Dino (*furiously*) You know something? You're a bitch!
Rupert I'm a professional. If my clients need bitching for their own good, then I bitch them.
Dino I am not your client!

Act II, Scene 2

Rupert We'll get a contract to you next week.
Dino And I'll treat it like these!

He strides to the table, snatches up photos, tears them across and throws them into the fireplace. He and Rupert look at each other

Rupert Very well. No Elsie. Then it'll have to be the Master Mariner. He's a bit small—but we can do something clever with a spotlight.
Dino You can't have that, either.
Rupert Why not?
Dino I'd never get permission.
Rupert You could ask.
Dino Would I be any use to you stone-deaf and half-paralysed?
Rupert Then you'll have to do something entirely new. Something large, spectacular—and preferably in oils.
Dino For God's sake! All this'd take forever!
Rupert (*quietly*) You've got seven weeks.
Dino Seven weeks ...!
Rupert This is April. It's a Summer exhibition.
Dino I will NOT give Henry and Elsie the satisfaction of seeing me work my guts out.
Rupert They needn't know you're working.
Dino Not know ...
Rupert You'll be surprised how much we can do once we start. Layout first, then you dictate the story and I'll type. The illustration can be worked up later. I promise you we can break the back of it this weekend.
Dino (*bitterly*) And the women win.
Rupert They won't know a thing till they read the reviews. You'll work at night——
Dino Rupert——
Rupert —and sleep during the day. Show yourself occasionally. They'll think you're sulking and sweating it out. Actually, they'll be doing the perspiring.
Dino They'll see all the stuff going out——
Rupert We'll collect that at night, too. In a plain van. Absolutely hush-hush. Everything will go like clockwork.
Dino Until I crawl down to the village and lay my laurels—if any—at Elsie's feet.

He turns back to the window. Rupert takes off her glasses and looks at him across the room

Rupert (*quietly*) Why are you so afraid of success?
Dino (*turning*) I won't be motivated. And I won't have people trying to tell me I'm a genius.
Rupert Don't flatter yourself. Genius comes seldom. You're trained—you can draw. A clean characteristic line. You have imagination and an outstanding sense of colour——
Dino So have millions of others.

Rupert They don't have me for an agent. And I'm staking my not-inconsiderable reputation that you could be a commercial success.
Dino (*scornfully*) Commercial!
Rupert It's a very comfortable word.

A pause

Well . . . ?
Dino I might consider the paintings. There isn't time for the book.
Rupert (*blowing up*) For God's sake, Dino—I'm not asking you to re-write the Encyclopaedia Britannica! This is a children's book, don't you understand? A book for *kids*. (*Gesturing*) Twelve by eight. Bright dust-jacket. Say four full-colour pages and six black and white—plus chapter headings and endpieces——
Dino Rupert——
Rupert We'll include six poems——(*She brings some stapled sheets from her briefcase*). "Daffodils"—no, we decided against that.
Dino (*suddenly belligerent*) What's wrong with it? (*He strides across to the table*)
Rupert Nothing. I just thought Wordsworth said it all. "Bluebell Wood". We'll use that. Most kids have never seen a bluebell wood and probably never will. "The Tree Prayer"—definitely. And "The Scarecrow". "The Robin". (*Looking up*) Yes, but you'll have to alter his feet.
Dino Why should I alter *anything*?
Rupert "The angry robin stamps his wire feet, and whistles shrilly with the wind." (*Crossing out*) Not *wire* feet. Bad image, and perhaps a bit twee——
Dino Now, look——
Rupert Actually we don't need the word at all. (*Scribbling*) "The angry robin stamps his feet, and whistles shrilly . . ." It doesn't alter the rhythm.
Dino You'll put "The angry robin stamps *impatient* feet, and whistles"—that doesn't alter the rhythm either.
Rupert Fine—fine. (*Writing*) "Impatient feet". (*Looking up*) You see how fast we can go if you co-operate?
Dino I only said——

Rupert brings out another page

Rupert Oh this—"The Wild White Horses". Eric's got an idea about putting this to music.
Dino A song . . . ?
Rupert For schools. "The Wild White Horses that live in the foam"—it goes perfectly into six-eight time.
Dino By God—you work fast . . .
Rupert Seven weeks, Dino. Seven weeks. Now—the story? Where is it?
Dino Story . . . ?
Rupert Not more than a hundred printed pages. Clear simple story. Clear bold type. For the fives to eights. Fantasy if you like, but not a fairy tale. By that age they're beginning to recognize reality.
Dino I haven't thought about a story.
Rupert Think about it now. Think of a title. The story might follow. Come

Act II, Scene 2

on Dino—say something. Anything. Off the top of your head. Come *on*, Dino—a title. Use your brains! A title, Dino! Think!

Dino (*suddenly*) *Arthur's Wall.*

Rupert *Arthur's Wall*—well, why not? Yes, this might be it. Arthur—sad little handicapped boy who makes it in the end. By God—if you got this right, the kids'd take him to their hearts.

Dino If you think——

Rupert Let's look at it. (*She inserts a sheet of paper into the typewriter*) Your title page. This is vitally important. Get their attention right away for what follows. So—thick bold caps—*Arthur's Wall.* And underneath—another poem—introductory—to connect it all in.

Dino I can't——

Rupert Come *on*, Dino. It isn't deathless verse. One of your little jingles. Something they can remember—and recite. Something that tells the story. Come on Dino—the story. Tell me a tale.

Dino (*slowly*) This is the tale—of Arthur's Wall . . .

Rupert (*typing rapidly*) Go on—go on.

Dino (*gaining confidence*) This is the tale of Arthur's Wall—built for him—when he was small . . .

Rupert Yes . . .

Dino But when he got older—it started to moulder, And now it isn't there at all.

Rupert (*typing madly*) Keep going, buddy boy! Keep going . . . !

CURTAIN

ACT III

Scene 1

A month later. Late evening

The chintz curtains at the windows and entrances C *and* L *have been replaced by some handsome patterned ones; the line over the fireplace has been removed; a pleasant oblong painting hangs on the wall* L *below the entrance to the staircase. The dresser is neat, with glasses, cups etc. tidily stacked. The window seat has also been recovered in a plain material, but the old cushions remain. A bright fire burns in the grate. The telephone is back on the window seat*

The table is centre, fully extended, covered by a white cloth with a deep lace border; a bowl of fruit and nuts, a decanter of brandy, glasses, dessert plates and linen napkins. Soft music plays in the background from the radio gradually fading

Henry sits L *back to the window. She wears a striking long red dress, long-sleeved, high-necked, with a large antique gold brooch. Merry sits* R *opposite; he wears a black suit and clerical collar but with a smart grey pleated vest. The Admiral has a black suit, soft pleated shirt and black bow tie. The effect is elegant without being over-formal. They are laughing and talking*

Mrs Morris enters R, *carrying a silver tray, with silver coffee pot, cream jug small cups and saucers. She is very trim in a black dress, white collar and cuffs and a small frilled waist apron—but the inevitable pansy hat*

Mrs Morris Here's your coffee . . .
Merry (*getting up*) May I take that . . .

He takes the tray and goes to Henry, passing behind the Admiral. He sets the tray in front of her and she pours coffee for the Admiral. Merry passes it while she pours a cup for him and he stands drinking it. This action does not interrupt the dialogue

Mrs Morris I brought it black, but there's cream for the Vicar if he wants it.
Merry Thank you.
Admiral Congratulations, Mrs Morris. Surpassed yourself. Splendid meal.
Mrs Morris As to that, sir, Miss Henry arranged it all. I just helped to cook it.
Henry But——
Mrs Morris Not that I wouldn't be able, as you very well know, sir——
Admiral I certainly should after so long——

Act III, Scene 1

Mrs Morris But when you leave school at fifteen for what used to be called good service—and then twenty years at the House with her Ladyship always that particular about everything——
Henry Thank you, Mrs Morris. Would you like to leave the washing up till the morning——
Mrs Morris (*indignant*) You know that would never be *my* way. And what did I bring Delia along for?
Henry Oh yes—I forgot about Delia. Is she all right?
Mrs Morris (*grimly*) She'd better be.

She marches out R

Henry (*laughing*) Oh, dear . . .
Merry But we really are lucky to have her. (*He goes back to his place carrying his cup, and sits down*)
Admiral Modern independence. Even the elders. Old days, they touched their hats to you, you touched your hat to them. Mutual respect.
Merry (*quietly*) Ideas change.
Admiral Not ideas. Standards. Take us three here. Decently dressed, elegant table, silver. What's the present style? Mugs on a formica top. Gane and me in dirty jeans—Henrietta with a tatty blouse open half-way down to her navel.
Henry Not just yet, I hope. Merry—a little more brandy?
Merry No thank you. I must look in on old Muxworthy on the way home.
Admiral (*quietly*) Going out with the tide is he?
Merry I think so.
Henry Shall you—stay with him?
Merry If they ask me. (*Slowly*) This is the particular occasion on which one feels so—inadequate.
Henry Inadequate? The privilege of holding someone's hand, and soothing them out of life?
Merry I hadn't quite thought of it like that. Privilege. Of course. (*Quietly*) Thank you.
Admiral Lonely business, dying. Lonely business living, if it comes to that. (*He drinks his brandy*)
Henry Not if one has plenty of interests. Admiral, will you do something for me?
Admiral Have one of these walnuts—here, I'll crack it for you. (*He does so*) Now, what must I do?
Henry You're Chairman of the Cottage Hospital Committee. Will you—pull a string?
Admiral How hard and what for?
Henry A quick in and out for Arthur. Otherwise he'll wait months.
Admiral Arthur? Delia's boy. Father unknown.
Henry (*quietly*) Actually, he was a traveller in wines and spirits.
Merry What . . . ?
Henry He went into the shop one lunchtime, thinking it was licensed. It seems he had a case of samples, rows of tiny coloured bottles. Nips he called them.

Admiral So they took a quick nip there and then——(*He breaks off, putting his hand over Henry's*) I beg your pardon. That was bad taste.
Merry Did Delia tell you this?
Henry Gradually. This is in the strictest confidence—but I thought you two should know.
Admiral Fellow must have been a swine. Taking advantage of that poor little rabbit.
Merry And everyone blames Willy Flagg.
Admiral Nonsense. Flagg's a decent chap. He'd have acknowledged the boy. Even if he is retarded.
Henry Not retarded. Deaf.
Merry Deaf . . . ?
Henry I had my suspicions. His eyes are too lively for a retarded child. I took him into Plymouth. Ostensibily to see a Disney film. Peripheral deafness. All he needs is adenoids and tonsils removed.
Merry But if it's peripheral——
Henry He gets about one word in ten. And no-one understands. So—frustration—screaming—making puddles——
Admiral Denis Calcroft. That's the man. Senior Consultant. I'll ring him tomorrow.
Henry Oh, thank you. If necessary I would pay a private fee——
Admiral (*angrily*) You will not! What do we pay our taxes for? When I think of my last assessment——
Henry ⎰ (*together* Now. Admiral . . .
Merry ⎱ *quickly*) We should all be very grateful . . .
Admiral Then see it goes to my credit in Heaven. Incidentally, not a bad attendance on Sunday. What was it? Twenty-four—twenty-five . . . ?
Henry Twenty-nine, actually. The Bennetts were a great help—so many of them . . .
Admiral You'd get a lot more coming if you stopped tampering with Holy Writ.
Henry (*quickly*) Now, Admiral . . .
Merry You know perfectly well it only goes back to the first Elizabethans.
Admiral Who did a superb job. Why do you come along after four hundred years, and mess it all up?
Merry It must be simplified so that people understand it.
Admiral You don't simplify it all that much. Take psalm one-o-seven—oh, yes, I know—it's one of my favourites. Prove my point—give us your revised version——
Henry Please. Let's not——
Admiral No—listen. Go on. Gane—"They that go down . . ."
Merry "Others there are who go to the sea in ships and make their living on the wide waters. These men have seen the way of the Lord and His marvellous doings in the deep——"
Admiral Marvellous doings in the deep—pah! Pay attention. This very passage—I was talking to old Muxworthy—God bless him—and do you know what he said?
Merry Well . . . ?

Act III, Scene 1

Admiral He said—"The new parts aren't that much more simple. All they've done is take out the thunder and the glory." The thunder and the glory. How about that!
Merry But do they really understand——
Admiral What does it matter what they understand so long as they enjoy the shape of the words together?
Merry (*a little edgy*) That's all very well. I'll go so far as to admit——
Admiral (*starting to simmer*) You'll damn well——
Henry (*quietly, getting up*) More coffee, Admiral?
Admiral Thank you, my dear. (*To Merry*) You'll go so far as to listen to the original.

Henry straightens up from refilling his cup, standing on his R

Dear lady—have you a copy of the *proper* prayer book handy? And then you can read it to us, Gane. Magnificent stuff—"They that go down——"
Henry (*quietly*) "They that go down to the sea in ships and have their business in great waters. They see the works of the Lord and His wonders in the deep. For at His Word the stormy wind arises—which lifteth the waves thereof——"

The telephone rings. Henry puts down the coffee-pot

Excuse me ... (*She crosses to the telephone. On the phone*) Gull Cottage. ... Yes. ... Yes, he is ...

Merry straightens up

I'll tell him. ... Yes. ... Right away. (*Putting down the telephone*) They want you to go.
Merry Thank you. (*Getting up*) Good-night, sir. (*He goes to the door* R)
Admiral Good-night. Oh, Gane—(*gruffly*)—tell the family, will you—anything I can do ...
Merry Of course.

Henry meets him in the doorway R

Thank you for—a very important evening. I'll remember what you said.
Henry I'll see you out. Excuse me Admiral.

She and Merry go out R

The Admiral pours another cup of coffee and goes to the window. He stands looking out and drinking

Mrs Morris enters R

Mrs Morris Beg pardon, sir. Have we finished with the tray?
Admiral Yes, thank you.

He finishes his coffee and holds out the cup. She takes it to the table and collects all other things on to the tray. A car is heard driving away off L

Mrs Morris Vicar's gone already, then?
Admiral Had an urgent phone call.

Mrs Morris Ah. Will I leave the brandy on the dresser?
Admiral By all means.

She takes the decanter and glasses to the dresser, returns c and picks up the tray

Mrs Morris Old Muxworthy, is it?
Admiral Looks like it.
Mrs Morris Ah, well, 'twas overdue. Born and bred in the village, and ninety-three last June. (*She crosses* R) It'll be a big funeral. Brighten up the week.

She goes out R

Admiral (*under his breath*) Good God ...

Henry enters R

Mrs Morris fetched the tray. I took the liberty of saying she could leave the brandy ...
Henry Quite right. Now—may I suggest you help me move the table and we can sit down comfortably for a last drink.
Admiral Certainly, where do you want it?
Henry By the window will do for now ...

They fold down both table flaps and move it in front of the window seat, leaving the cloth in place. Henry takes one upright chair L, *above the window seat. The Admiral moves the other two chairs* R *and* L *of the trolley, speaking as he crosses*

Admiral Gane all right?
Henry Of course. Why wouldn't he be?
Admiral Needs spiritual discipline.

He goes to the fireplace and sits on the green armchair. Henry sits opposite

No use being squeamish over deathbeds.
Henry Not squeamish. Sensitive.
Admiral Nor that, neither. (*Suddenly*) Good God, Henrietta, haven't I had to deal with it—hundreds of times—and at sea? On a board—wrapped in a flag—sound the bugles, tilt the board—"We now commit this body to the deep———" (*He stops suddenly. Quietly*) How many more times this evening am I to ask your pardon?
Henry (*smiling*) Have that last brandy.
Admiral (*glancing at his wristwatch*) And then I really have to go. Must tackle some paperwork before bed. Parish Council meeting tomorrow. And that bounder Foresdyke's got to be put in his place.
Henry Alas, poor Foresdyke. (*Getting up*) If you like to wait while I change my shoes I'll come down to the car with you.
Admiral Certainly not. All those steps and back again. And that damned handrail's still shaky.
Henry I'm used to both. And it's a beautiful night. There seem to be even more stars than usual.

Act III, Scene 1

She goes out C through the curtain

The Admiral goes to the dresser and pours his brandy. His back is to the room and he is partially screened by the door R as it opens

Delia enters R. She wears the flowered dress and fawn cardigan. Her hair has been cut and dressed, the effect ruined by a thick net covering it down to her eyebrows. She goes to the table by the window and puts a hand out to the cloth

The Admiral turns

Admiral (*genially*) 'Evening, Delia.

Delia freezes, then whips round, dragging the cloth off the table. Her free hand goes to her mouth

Have you had a good day?

She stands staring at him

Good heavens, girl! What's the matter? I'm not going to bite you. Here—let me help you with that . . .

She still stands motionless

Dammit, who d'you think I am? Dracula? Now come along—come along . . .

He takes a couple of steps forward. Delia makes a faint mewing sound behind her hand. The sudden ominous groaning and clanging sounds from L. The Lights start flashing frantically off and on

Henry (*off* C) Oh—NO! (*She is heard stumbling downstairs* C)
Admiral (*stopping*) Good God—what's happening!

A vivid flash and the stage blacks out. Confused voices

During the black-out, Henry enters C and Mrs Morris enters R

Henry ⎫   Find the hammer—get the hammer . . .
Mrs Morris ⎬ (*together*)   It's that dratted boiler—kick it?
Admiral ⎭   What the hell do we do—get a TORCH!

Three deafening metallic bangs off L. The Lights got up to full. Henry stands C in front of the curtain. The Admiral has moved C. Mrs Morris stands in the doorway R. They all stand in silence, staring L

Delia stands in front of the studio curtain, the tablecloth draped round her like a cloak. She grips a large heavy hammer in both hands

Mrs Morris (*whispering*) Delia——
Henry (*whispering*) Quiet.

Delia pauses. Then goes slowly across to the Admiral. He braces himself and faces her firmly. She stands and looks at him for a second. Then she reaches for his arm and pulls it out straight

Suddenly she thrusts the handle of the hammer into his hand, closes his fingers over it, and rushes out R, *past Mrs Morris, pulling the cloth over her head*

Mrs Morris (*faintly, all in one breath*) Oh-my-good-Gawd ... !

She goes out R, *shutting the door*

The Admiral drops the hammer in the hearth, pulls out a handkerchief and mops his forehead. Henry comes to the fireplace, smiling. She has a handsome black lace scarf draped round her shoulders. The Admiral takes his glass from the dresser

Henry Would it be too facetious to enquire if you've had an interesting evening?

Admiral One way and another—not a dull moment. (*He moves* C, *glass in hand*) In all seriousness—I've not enjoyed anything so much for a long time. Everything beautifully—and cleverly arranged. Excellent food—and this superb brandy! (*He raises his glass to her, drains it and puts it on the dresser*)

Henry A legacy from my uncle. You must come again sometime and we'll open another bottle.

She gives him her hand. He takes it in both of his own

Admiral But get that ruddy handrail strengthened first.

He opens the door R *for her and they go out laughing*

After a pause, Dino comes in L *from the studio, carrying a large sketch-pad and pencil. He stretches, yawns and shivers, then crosses to the fire, tucks the pad and pencil down by the side of the brown chair and puts a log on. Fireglow up. The phone rings*

Dino Oh, hell ... (*He goes to the phone*) Hallo? ... Oh—Rupert—for heaven's sake—I've only just got up. ... Of course I've been working—you've got your last batch of stuff, haven't you? ... What? ... The spectacular? ... No, I haven't ... No. ... Because I can't find a suitable subject, that's why. ... No—no—Rupert—don't NAG! I'll tell you what—find a really pretty calendar—kittens with bows—and blow it up to the right size. Everyone'll LOVE it! ... No—yes—all right—Rupert—don't CROWD ME! Good*bye*! (*He slams down the phone, moves to the fire, warms his hands and plugs in the kettle*)

A car drives off L

Henry enters R

Hallo, there. I thought you'd gone to bed.

Henry Just went down to see the Admiral off. (*She sits down in the green chair*) Dino—that handrail——

Dino I'll do it quietly tomorrow. Do you want some coffee?

Henry No, thank you.

The kettle boils. He makes a mug of coffee

Act III, Scene 1

The amount of coffee consumed in this house, we ought to consider growing our own.

Dino Cheaper than gin. And less harmful to the liver. (*He sits down in the brown chair*) How did your evening go?

Henry I think one might describe it as variegated and splendid.

Dino You're looking rather splendid yourself tonight. I like that black lace scarf. And all that stiff silk—the colour suits you. Mm—claret, I think. Yes—vintage claret—in a thin glass—held up against firelight.

Henry A relic of better days.

Dino Do you miss them? Sab once said "Henry is the power to Fabian's elbow."

Henry (*drily*) Very perceptive.

Dino Henry, old love, why did you and Fabian twine so long? So sterile for you. No husband, and your generation couldn't have affairs.

Henry Of course we had affairs, you silly child. We just didn't put them in the gossip columns of a leading daily newspaper.

Dino You surely *could* have married?

Henry That's a long and sordid story.

Dino Oh, do tell! Let's have a glorious unbosoming.

Henry (*laughing*) You sound like Rupert.

Dino Never! But I'll tell you what—if you'll reveal all, I might—only *might* mind—I just might do two sordid drawings for her.

Henry Three.

Dino Perhaps. So—give.

Henry (*slowly*) I was—just nineteen. Fresh out of college. Inordinately conceited and with considerably less knowledge of life than—than the average burying beetle.

Dino And you fell in love. No—don't tell me. With a distinguished elderly don. Was it a splash or a cataract?

Henry Niagara. A handsome hard-bitten Major in the Indian army. Twice my age, and with a very practised line in romantic seduction.

Dino I'm relieved the seduction was at least romantic.

Henry Oh yes. In those days, India was still glamorous. He even threw in the Taj by moonlight. And—(*pausing*)—I *did* so remind him of his poor dead wife.

Dino Oh—*no*!

Henry Killed in a tragic accident. Died in his arms murmuring "Find happiness with someone else."

Dino How *did* it end?

Henry He went back to his regiment. I was to follow. I was now of age. Everything arranged—my passage booked——

Dino And then—the letter arrived.

Henry (*quietly*) From the poor dead wife.

Dino Henry ... !

Henry A very pleasant reasonable letter. She was *so* sorry, but it was always happening. And she always forgave him. So did the two children. She *did* hope I would understand. And forget. And with best wishes, yours very sincerely.

Dino My poor love. What *did* you do?

Henry Oh, couldn't face my parents. Or my friends. I rushed to Fabian and wept on his shoulder. He took me to Greece for six months—to help him research a book.
Dino And so began the twining process. But surely—you were so young...
Henry I see now, that I settled into a most comfortable rut. We had a full and luxurious life. I also had the run of a very keen and cultivated mind.
Dino You ran his life. You were hostess, secretary and travelling companion. Why the hell didn't he provide for you?
Henry I still haven't worked that out yet. But as he never did anything without good reason—well, there it is... (*She gets up and takes his mug*) Now, you start drawing while I just rinse this——

A log shifts in the grate. The light catches her. Dino jumps up

Dino Henry—wait!
Henry What is it, dear?
Dino Sit down.
Henry But what——
Dino Don't argue. Here—give me that damned mug——(*he snatches it from her and puts it on the fireside cupboard*) Now—sit down——
Henry But——
Dino Sit down—sit down...! (*He pushes her into the chair*) Now—sit back. Relaxed. Turn your head left—chin up like you're listening.
Henry Dino——
Dino Hands in your lap. No—just clasp them loosely. God—that crimson against the green—why have I only just seen it! Wait—put that black lace thing over—no—I'll do it—(*He kneels down, arranging the scarf*)—round like that—and falling so the silk shows through... (*He stands up, and moves back looking at her*) That's it! That's absolutely it. Three-quarters. Life-size. (*He snatches up pad and pencil*) And I'll call it—"Portrait of a Gentlewoman". No—"Portrait of a Gentle Lady". Only we'll show you're not all gentle—there's steel underneath. Now sit while I rough it out.
Henry Dino—what are we doing?
Dino (*triumphantly*) I'm going to paint you, old Henry! And it'll be my masterpiece!

He is sketching rapidly as——

—*the* CURTAIN *falls*

SCENE 2

July. Early evening

The room is unchanged except that the table is back C

Mrs Morris, in her tweed skirt, a bright blouse and of course, the pansy hat, is polishing the top of the table. A busy typewriter can be heard off C. *The phone rings. Mrs Morris crosses and answers it*

Act III, Scene 2   55

Mrs Morris Gull Cottage.... Yes.... Oh, hallo, Vicar. Hold on—I'll ask. (*She puts down the phone and calls*) Miss Henry ...!
The typewriter continues. She crosses C *to the curtain*
    Miss Henry ...!
The typewriter stops
Henry (*off*) Yes ...?
Mrs Morris Tes Vicar. He's at station——
Henry Well, what does he——
Mrs Morris Says he wants to come straight over.
Henry Ask him if it's urgent.
Mrs Morris goes back to the phone
Mrs Morris She says is it urgent? (*She listens, the returns* C. *Calling*) It's urgent.
Henry All right. He can come.
Mrs Morris trots back to the phone
Mrs Morris She says come. Goodbye. (*She returns to polishing the table*)
The typewriter continues for a moment, then stops. Mrs Morris crosses to the window and pushes it up. Seagulls are heard. She shakes her duster out of the window and returns C, *folding it up*

   Henry enters C *wearing one of her smart dark dresses, and with her glasses on. She carries a long legal envelope and a small square one*

    I've put table back ...
Henry Thank you. He'd better find it here when he arrives. Though I don't know when.
Mrs Morris Nearly ten days, isn't it? People are wondering. What's he doing in London?
Henry I think he's gone to look at some pictures.
Mrs Morris I should have thought he'd got plenty of his own to look at—once they've had the dust blown off.
Henry Mrs M. would you be a dear and post this for me—it's rather urgent.
Mrs Morris (*taking the envelope*) It won't be off today.
Henry It will be off my mind. (*She gives Mrs Morris the small envelope*) And that's yours. I think you'll find it's right.
Mrs Morris It always is. You won't forget I'll not be here for a fortnight.
Henry Oh, yes. Fowey. How's your daughter coming along? Only about a week now, isn't it?
Mrs Morris That's what doctor says. Her—she were born slow and been slow ever since. Kept me waiting on overtime for nearly six weeks. (*She puts the folded duster in the dresser drawer*)
Henry The Admiral's going to miss you.
Mrs Morris He's managed before. The freezer's full—all home-cooked. And Elsie'll look in if she can ...

Merry hurries in R *carrying a large bundle of folded newspapers*

Merry Henry—oh, hallo, Mrs M. How are you?
Mrs Morris So long as I'm standing up you needn't bother to ask. I'll put this in for you——
Henry Thank you.
Mrs Morris —but it'll likely lie till Monday.

She hurries out R

Henry (*calling*) I hope it's a boy!
Merry Have you seen your *Telegraph* this morning?
Henry As a matter of fact, no. It doesn't get up here till midday, and I haven't had time. (*Looking round*) Did you want it ...?
Merry No, I've got two among this lot ... (*He puts the bundle on the table and pulls out two folded papers*)
Henry Merry—what's all this?
Merry You knew I've been in Plymouth all day—well, I bought a lunchtime edition and when I read it I thought I'd better buy up all the others I could. Here's your *Telegraph*. (*He gives her the paper and opens his own copy*) Arts Section. Page Three.
Henry Arts ... (*She opens out the paper. Reading*) "New arrival at Braganza." "London welcomes fresh talent——"
Merry (*reading*) "Rupert Dominic, publisher and entrepreneur, has brought off a pleasing double at the Braganza Gallery, with an exhibition of paintings and the publication of a charming children's book——"
Henry (*reading*) "—of a charming children's book called *Arthur's Wall*, both the work of a newcomer, Dino Ellis——"
Merry "The reproduction of the mural, the Wall, is a clever touch, but the interest lies in the paintings—particularly the portrait technique, which shows an interesting delineation of character..." (*He pauses and pulls out another newspaper*) Here's this bit in *The Guardian*. Listen ...

He reads. Henry reads over his shoulder

"Mr Ellis is not yet a Gainsborough, but with hard work and discipline, he may surprise us."
Henry "In any case, he appears to have an uncanny gift of painting one character and revealing another ..." "(*Looking up*) I said so!
Merry (*reading*) "For example, in the striking canvas: "Portrait of a Gentle Lady"——

Elsie rushes in R, *trailing a newspaper in her hand. She is considerably distressed*

Elsie Miss Henry——!
Henry Oh, Elsie, you know. Where did you get——
Elsie Someone left it behind lunchtime. I only just got to pick it up——
Henry Isn't it splendid——
Elsie Splendid! (*Throwing the paper on the table*) Oh, Miss Henry, we should never have done it——

Act III, Scene 2

Henry Why, Elsie——
Elsie I shouldn't have agreed—I thought just a book—something simple—a bit more money here and there. And now he's famous——
Henry Elsie——
Elsie —do you think he'll be bothered with me?
Henry Now listen——
Elsie Why did we have to start it. I ought to have known ... (*She puts her hands over her face*)
Henry (*putting an arm round her*) If you'll just calm down——
Elsie (*shaking her off*) Go away ...!

She turns to run C. *Merry stops her*

Merry Elsie, I'm not at all clear what this is about myself, but I'm sure Dino wouldn't——
Henry Listen. No—listen——(*She pulls Elsie's hands from her face*) To begin with, he isn't famous.
Elsie It's in the paper.

A car is heard faintly off R

Henry You mustn't take too much notice. It's just a beginning, and it may never happen again. These things blow up and they blow over——
Elsie But——
Henry —but I do think he'll get established, if only in a small way, and then if he'll work you'll have a little money for the little things you want——
Elsie He won't want *me*.
Merry I don't think you're being very fair to him——

Dino's excited voice calls off R

Dino (*off*) Elsie! Henry! Where are you! Anybody home!

He bursts in R, *elated, on top of the world. He carries a number of bags marked "Fortnum and Mason"—and one labelled "Tesco"*

I'm BACK! Move over! Look at all this! (*He sweeps the papers from the table and bangs down the bags*) We're going to have a banquet! Rupert can keep Harrods ...!
Henry Dino!

Dino pulls a bottle of champagne from one of the bags and begins to twist the wire

Dino Elsie—get the glasses ...

Elsie does not move. Merry glances at her, then fetches four glasses from the dresser. Dino does not stop talking

I'll buy up London tomorrow—didn't have time today. Elsie we're rich—do you hear. All the wealth of the Indies—here everybody—here ...

The cork pops. He pours wine into glasses, and pushes a glass into Elsie's hand. She moves abruptly to the window and puts the glass on the sill. Dino raises his glass

Move over Lord Hanson! The world isn't yours any more!

They all drink except Elsie

Look at this then . . . ! (*He empties the Tesco bag on to the table. Wads of notes in elastic bands fall out*)

Henry (*together*) Dino . . . !
Merry Oh, my God . . .

Dino Look at it! Thick as leaves in Valombrosa—and plenty more left on the tree! (*He scoops up a bundle of packets and throws them in the air*) Yippee!
Merry Dino . . . ! (*He puts down his glass and picks up some of the packets*)
Dino Leave it—leave it! Have some more champagne. (*He refills glasses*) Now—(*he pushes a pile of packets towards Henry*)—there you are, Henry. That's for you.
Henry Dino——

He pushes another pile over to Merry

Dino And there's yours, Merry.
Merry But——
Dino Give it to the church if you must. Mothers' Union—or some little peppermints for the choirboys.
Henry If you could just be sane for one moment——
Dino Why? The world is mad and I'm mad. We're all mad—and it's *wonderful*! Now . . . (*He brings some parcels from another carrier*) Specials—for my special people. (*He gives Henry an oblong gift-wrapped package*) Henry—yours. And Merry—(*he gives Merry a flat package*)—for you. Go on—open them. Elsie, love, the tiniest little thing for you. (*He goes to her with a small uninteresting little parcel in a brown paper bag*) Here . . . (*He puts it into her unresponsive hand and returns to the table* C)
Henry Dino, why . . . ? (*She has opened her parcel and holds a gold bracelet*)
Dino Because you had to sell your old one. Replacement.

Merry is holding a thin leather book

Merry Dino—you can't mean this——
Dino You old fool I know you've been lusting for a really good copy ever since you were ordained.
Merry (*quietly*) Nicholas de Montez—*The Meditations*.
Dino Only the eighteen-sixty edition. I couldn't get you the original. It's in the Amsterdam Museum. (*He finishes his champagne and turns*) Elsie, what about yours . . . ?

Elsie has opened the bag. She still stands facing the window, holding a small square leather case. Dino goes to her

Here—put it on. (*He takes the case, opens it and takes out the ring. He puts the case in his pocket. He lifts her left hand and puts the ring on the third finger*) If you don't like it, we'll get it changed. But you did once say you liked emeralds.

Act III, Scene 2

He returns to the table. Elsie does not move

We'll see about the gold one later. Merry, you'll "do" us, won't you. Personally, I'd prefer the registrar, but I expect the village will want a spectacle. Lord—I suppose I'll need a best man. (*Laughing*) Damned if I don't ask the Master Mariner——

There is a dead silence. Elsie does not move. Henry and Merry stand at each end of the table, looking down. Dino drains his glass and reaches for the bottle. He pauses, the atmosphere reaching him at last. He looks at them, then over at Elsie, then back at them. He puts down the bottle and crosses to Elsie. He turns her to face him, and takes her hands

(*Quietly*) Elsie, my love—my morning star . . . (*He goes down on his knees in front of her*) Will you marry me?

Elsie stands looking down at him. Suddenly she pulls her hands away, breaks into quiet but anguished sobs and rushes off C

(*Getting up*) Elsie! Elsie!

He runs C. *Merry stops him*

Merry Dino——
Dino Damn you—let me alone!
Merry (*firmly*) Dino—not now!
Dino For God's sake—what did I say? What did I DO!
Merry Just give her a little time.
Henry (*collecting money up*) Dino, I can't possibly take this.
Dino Brace yourself. You're getting a lot more.
Henry Why . . . ?
Dino Your picture's been sold. I'm giving you half.
Henry Dino, who bought it?
Dino No-one knows.
Henry Impossible. Someone somewhere must have signed something.
Dino All done through an agent. Very cloak and dagger. Fortunately we're allowed to keep it till we close.
Henry I *would* like to know where it's going.
Dino Oh, Rupert says it'll turn up somewhere. It's not valuable enough to lock up in a vault. So take your share and don't argue. What will you do with it?
Henry I do have some plans simmering. I can't stay here for ever.
Dino Don't you dare leave us. She's our luckpiece, isn't she, Merry?
Merry (*laughing*) Not only ours. I met Arthur on the way up, and he told me—with the utmost clarity and a sweet smile—to blank blank get out of his blank blank way.
Henry How absolutely splendid . . . !

Elsie comes C *through the curtain, pulling on a thin summer coat. She crosses* R

Dino Elsie—where're you going?

Elsie (*turning*) Where do you think I'm going? To work, of course.
Dino My wife is not pulling any more pints in any crummy pub!
Elsie Oh, changed your mind, have you? Got too big to marry a barmaid?
Dino You don't need to be a barmaid. (*He indicates the money*) Not with all this——
Elsie And how long do you think *all this* is going to last?
Dino Elsie——
Elsie I know you, Dino Ellis. You're already throwing it around like confetti—wine and presents—and all that rich messed-up food. You'll never stop till you suddenly find it's all gone.
Dino You——
Elsie And then we'll be back where we started. We'll get it all scrapped up and put in the bank until Miss Henry's Mr Charles advises us what to do with it. Until then, something's got to keep coming in regular.
Dino (*angrily*) I forbid you to go down to *The Lobster* tonight!
Elsie Oh, *do* you? And how much longer do you think I can wait to show 'em all this!

She waves her left hand dramatically in the air and runs out R. *The door slams*

Dino Did you hear that! She's been nagging me for years to make some money—and when I do she won't spend it!
Henry She *is* right, Dino. How much is actually here?
Dino Oh, *I* don't know. Rupert gave me a draft on the bank and I asked for sovereigns—but the cashier just raised his eyebrows and said "Yes, sir. Fives, tens or twenties." (*He pours a last drink*)
Merry May I take it home and put it in the strongbox with the church funds? I don't have a safe, but it would be more secure there than here.
Dino For heaven's sake, Merry, do what you like. It's only money—not blood.

He drinks. Henry pushes some packets across the table

Henry Room for mine, too?
Merry Of course. (*He collects the packets into the Tesco carrier, and ties up the handles*)

A car is heard approaching L *at break-neck speed*

Henry Hallo, we've got a visitor ...
Dino Perhaps it's Elsie coming back. (*He goes to the window and leans out*) Elsie, is that you, my love?
Admiral (*off* L) No, it is NOT your love, as you're very soon going to find out ... (*His voice fades*)
Dino (*closing the window*) It's the Admiral. Were we expecting him? I wonder what he wants——

The Admiral bursts in R. *He is in a tremendous rage*

Admiral What the bloody hell d'you mean by this?
Henry Admiral—what *is* the matter?

Act III, Scene 2   61

Dino Here—better have a drink——
Admiral You can take your damned drink and pour it down your damned drain. I've never been so insulted in my life!
Henry If you would just calm down and tell us what you're talking about——
Admiral Talking about! Talking about! As if you didn't know!
Dino Know what?
Admiral Are you going to tell me you haven't seen your television this evening?
Dino We don't have a television. What should we have looked at?
Admiral For one thing—my face!
Henry What——!
Dino Your——?
Admiral Leering out of the screen—and a bunch of moon-faced pansies drooling—and a label. "Old Polaris"!
Dino (*whispering*) Oh, my God——
Admiral Arts programme—item slipped in. Me—a laughing stock, and the pansies rabbitting on—magnificent—masterpiece. Picture of the year . . . ! Picture of the year . . . !
Henry There must be some mistake.
Admiral And as for you, Henrietta—how could you do it? I thought better of you——
Dino Admiral, give me a moment——
Admiral I'll give you nothing but notice to quit. You're an unprincipled young layabout and you want a damn good hiding!
Henry (*topping him*) Edward . . . !

There is a sudden silence

(*Quietly*) I should *think* so. Roaring away like that. Now—I assure you there has been some mistake. We knew nothing about this.
Dino Your picture should not have been there. And certainly never hung without permission. Now, if you'll excuse me, I'm going to ring Rupert.

He unplugs the phone and goes L *into the studio*

Henry So if you'll sit down——
Admiral I'll stand, thank you, ma'am. And you'll get that picture removed. And destroyed. Before I get an injunction . . .
Henry What did you mean by giving Dino notice to quit?
Admiral It's my cottage. I've been fool enough to let him have it all these years—at a peppercorn rent . . .
Merry Come, be fair. He's made it habitable——
Admiral You keep quiet, Gane. Getting mixed up in this. You're a disgrace to your cloth——
Merry (*suddenly*) You will not speak to me like that!
Henry (*quickly breaking in*) Merry is not mixed up in anything. If anyone motivated this I did.
Admiral Then you should be ashamed of yourself. Sitting at my table. Borrowing my books. And making me a figure of fun.

Henry I have done nothing of the kind! You are not to say that——
Admiral ⎫　　　　　　　I'll say what I damn well——
Henry　⎬ (*together*)　You're behaving disgracefully——
Merry ⎭　　　　　　　Stop it, you two! Stop it!

Dino enters L

Dino I've spoken to Rupert.
Admiral I don't want to hear——
Henry You'll listen. Yes, Dino . . . ?
Dino It's that arts programme. Called Top Spot. They came in in the morning, on impulse. Film everything live, and put it on just after the six o'clock news . . .
Henry But how did——
Dino Just before they arrived this morning, two pictures were sold. One of the assistants found "Old—" found the Admiral's picture in a box marked "replacements".
Henry But it shouldn't have been there.
Dino No. It was a mistake when we packed. Admiral, I couldn't be more sorry——
Admiral You'll be sorrier still before I've finished.
Henry But didn't Rupert know?
Dino She's been away all day—in Sussex. I just caught her as she got back. Admiral I do assure you—it will be all right——
Admiral It is NOT all right! No-one is going to make a public fool of *me*. You've got twenty-eight days to vacate this place. Understand?
Merry Admiral——
Admiral Twenty-eight days. And I'm handing the whole thing over to my solicitors. Good evening.

He strides out R

Henry Come back, you pig-headed old idiot!
Admiral (*retreating, off* R) I'll thank you not to call me names, ma'am. (*Fainter*) I've said my last word and I'm standing by it——

He shouts loudly. There is a splintering sound and a crash

　Bloody hell!
Henry Oh my God—that handrail! He's gone down the cliff path! (*She starts to cross* R) All right. Admiral—I'm coming . . .
Dino No, Henry—wait! Come on, Merry . . .

He and Merry run off R. *Dino is heard calling*

(*off*) Hold on, Admiral—hold on . . . !

Voices and confusion are heard R, *moving to* L. *Henry goes to the window and pushes it up. Seagulls are heard, getting fainter*

Admiral (*now off* L) That'll do—that'll do! Stop fiddling and fussing—can't you!
Merry (*off*) If you'll let us——

Act III, Scene 2

The Admiral gives a sudden shout of real pain

Admiral (*off*) That's enough, damn you! Get me on my feet!
Henry (*calling*) Dino—what's happened?
Dino (*off, calling*) Luckily he fell just above the break . . .
Henry Can you get him back up here?
Dino (*off, calling*) Have to—no other way—We'll get him up——
Admiral (*off*) You'll do nothing of the sort! Get me down into the car——

Confusion is heard off L. The Admiral shouting, Merry and Dino apparently trying to lift him. Henry goes C, pushes the table slightly out of the way and brings the green chair forward C. She shakes up the cushion and brings another cushion from the window seat. Noises appear to move to R

Dino (*off* R) Now take it easy, Admiral. We're only trying to help . . .

Dino and Merry enter R, supporting the Admiral between them. He has his arms round their shoulders and is struggling and hopping on his left leg

Admiral It's all your damned fault in the first place. I've told you over and again to get that blasted deathtrap mended. I'll sue you for damages.

They sit him down in the armchair

Henry Now you just be quiet—and reasonable—for a moment. (*She kneels down and very gently feels his right leg*)
Admiral Take your hands off me, woman, and let me up. I'm going home—
—(*He breaks off*)
Henry You're not going anywhere for the moment. It looks as though your ankle's broken. Dino—phone for an ambulance.
Dino Sure.

He goes off L into the studio

Admiral I am NOT going in any blasted ambulance. (*He moves incautiously, swears under his breath and is silent*)
Henry Will they get a stretcher up, do you think?
Merry We'll have to see. I think if we can carry him down below the break—but we couldn't leave him where he was——
Admiral I told you to get me down into the car——
Merry Quite impossible. The next thing to do is to make a temporary repair——
Dino (*off* L) Merry! Can you give me a hand . . .
Merry Coming.

He goes off L into the studio

Admiral If you want to be really helpful, you can give me a spot of that brandy . . .
Henry I'm sorry—no. It would be most inadvisable.
Admiral I'll judge what's advisable. What's wrong with a little brandy against shock.
Henry We can't risk it before a general anaesthetic.

Admiral (*now considerably quieter*) General ...? What the hell d'you mean? I've probably only twisted a muscle. Doctor can come in and strap it up ...
Henry We'll see what they say at the hospital.
Admiral I'm NOT going to hospital.
Henry Don't be so awkward. Why do you think Dino's rung for an ambulance.
Admiral I'm not going in any ambulance, either ... (*He starts to move up in the chair, puts his injured right foot to the ground and pauses. He slowly eases himself back again, takes out a handkerchief and wipes his forehead*)
Henry (*gently*) Now, you see? So just sit quiet and still while I try and ease that foot. (*She fetches another cushion from the window seat and kneels down by the chair*) Now—hang on ...

The Admiral grips the arms of the chair. Very carefully, Henry slips the cushion under his right foot and gets up

Well done. Now we'll get you a couple of pain killers.

Dino and Merry enter L. *Dino carries a coil of rope and some lengths of wood. Merry has a spade*

Dino Ambulance'll be up in ten minutes.

He goes out R

Merry (*pausing by the chair*) How are you feeling now, Admiral?

The Admiral merely growls under his breath

(*To Henry*) Anything I can do here before we get busy on the path?
Henry Oh, Merry please. Will you find three codeine in the kitchen cupboard—and bring a glass of water ...
Merry Sure.

He props the spade against the trolley and goes out R

Admiral I'm not taking that chemists' muck.
Henry Oh, please don't start being awkward again.
Admiral Once and for all—I'm going home.
Henry I expect they'll keep you in for the night. Then if you insist——
Admiral I'll discharge myself.
Henry That's your privilege. But once you're home, have you thought what you'll do when you get there?
Admiral Ring Mrs Morris. She'll cope.
Henry She's in Fowey—remember? Her daughter's having a baby.
Admiral Damned inconvenient girl.
Henry So you'll just have to rely on the District Nurse.
Admiral I'll not have that woman near me! Face like a boot.
Henry (*laughing*) So she has. A nice comfortable brown brogue. But we needn't tell her. And she is most efficient——
Admiral Will you kindly stop trying to arrange my life?
Henry Must you be so—so dramatic—and Victorian ...

Act III, Scene 2

Merry enters R, carrying a small glass filled with cloudy liquid
Oh, thank you, Merry. If you'll just give it to him. I've remembered something upstairs ...
She goes off C through the curtain
Merry holds out the glass to the Admiral
Merry Here you are, then. Soluble. I've shaken it up well.
Admiral (*now quiet, but indomitable*) Take the blasted stuff away.
Merry Now, Admiral——
Admiral If you want to make yourself useful, get me a tot of brandy while that managing woman's out of the way.
Merry You know I can't do that. Take this. It's hardly a Micky Finn, but it will dull the pain a bit.
Admiral Stop waving it under my nose and take yourself off. Who do you think you are, telling me what to do——
Merry (*suddenly raising his voice*) Shut up and drink it down!
A pause. They look at each other
Admiral (*quietly*) By God, Gane, you wouldn't dare speak to me like that if I were on my feet.
Merry (*also quiet*) Well, you're not.
Admiral I see. Kick a man when he's down.
Merry It's the only time you'll listen.
Admiral Go away. I'm tired of you. (*He leans back and closes his eyes*)
Merry Not so tired as I am of you.
Admiral (*opening his eyes*) Hey——?
Merry I didn't particularly want to come to this remote village. I go where I'm sent, to do my best for the community. You're a leading figure here. You've got influence and authority. We ought to work together.
Admiral I——
Merry Don't interrupt. I know you liked Wainwright, and you'll probably never like me. But if you stopped shouting and laying down the law—and showed a little understanding, it might be better for all of us. Including you. (*He holds out the glass*) So drink this.
The Admiral looks at him for a second. Then he takes the glass, drains it and hands it back
Admiral Thank 'ee. I'm obliged. (*He pulls out his handkerchief and wipes his lips*)
Merry puts the glass on the dresser
Merry And you can stop calling me Gane.
Admiral What ...
Merry (*coming back to the chair*) I'm not your gamekeeper, nor your gardener, nor your dog. I don't suggest you get to "Merry" right away. But you could make a start by calling me Vicar.
Henry comes in C carrying a thick expensive travelling rug

Henry I remembered this—it was Fabian's. Oh, good—you've taken the codeine. You didn't give Merry any trouble, did you?
Merry (*straight-faced*) Took it like an officer and a gentleman.

He collects the spade and goes out R

Henry shakes out the rug and tucks it round the Admiral

Admiral What're you trying to do now? Suffocate me?
Henry You need warmth after shock. Surely you know that. Now—I've been thinking——
Admiral (*under his breath*) Oh, God——
Henry You won't be able to use the stairs for a while. So we'll bring your bed down into the library. Merry will look in each day. And Elsie when she can. And once you get your elbow crutches——
Admiral You seem determined to drive me into a corner.
Henry Not at all. You make all the decisions. (*Meekly*) Might I ask you to let me have the little gable room?
Admiral I'll——
Henry You'll need to be quiet for a day or two. Plenty of rest, and small light meals. (*Thoughtfully*) A little fish——
Admiral (*bitterly*) Steamed, I suppose. Damned pap.
Henry Certainly not. Grilled—with lemon juice and a little mayonnaise. And I make a rather special creamed apple soufflé—I got the recipe in Texas. And some nice fresh rolls—and some of your favourite Brie——
Admiral Do stop going on about food!
Henry Food is very important during the convalescent period——
Admiral Henrietta——
Henry Did you know I play a quite a fair game of chess——
Admiral Henrietta——
Henry Fabian taught me. He was an expert of course, as he was in everything——
Admiral (*slightly raising his voice*) Henrietta!
Henry (*meekly*) Yes, Admiral?
Admiral (*quietly*) It wouldn't work, you know. We can't be together ten minutes without shouting at each other.
Henry Then we must either control ourselves or learn to enjoy it.

An ambulance bell is heard off L

Oh, good. They're here ...

She goes to the window and looks out. Voices heard off L

(*Calling*) Dino! What happens now?
Dino (*off, calling*) Just a minute ...

Pause. Discussion is heard faintly off L

(*Off*) They say get him half-way and they'll take over. Hold on—we're coming up!
Henry Right. (*She shuts the window and turns* C, *removes the rug and folds it*)

Act III, Scene 2

There you are. Nothing more to worry about. Just be sensible and leave it all to them. (*She puts the rug on the table*)

Dino and Merry enter R

Dino Ready, Admiral? Hospital's been alerted. We're going straight to X-Ray . . .

They start to lift him carefully between them

Admiral It's to be clearly understood I'm not staying more than one night.
Merry You can fight that out when we get there. Now—up you come. Careful!

Henry kneels down and eases the cushion from under his foot. They get him upright and take him to the door R. *Dino calls through the door*

Dino Here we are, boys. We've got him . . .

They ease the Admiral out R. *An ambulance man's voice is heard*

Man (*off*) Evenin' sir. We'll have you all right and tight in a jiffy. No—leave it to us. (*Fainter*) Watch it, lads. Keep to the right at the broken corner.

More voices and bustle are now heard off L

Henry takes the Fortnum's bags down to the trolley, pushes the green chair back into place and takes the cushions to the window seat. She stands looking out of the window, listening for a second, then returns to the table, collects the folded rug and goes out C *through the curtain*

Voices and bustle die away. The ambulance bell clangs off into the distance

Henry returns C, *wearing a light coat and carrying her handbag and a small case, which she puts on table. She opens the case, removes packets of notes from the Tesco bag, fits them neatly into the case, adds her bracelet in its box and Merry's book, and shuts the lid*

Dino comes in R *carrying the spade. He crosses* L *to the curtain and puts it behind, talking all the time*

Dino (*cheerfully*) Well, that's fixed that. Merry's gone in the ambulance, so we can follow in his car. (*Turning* C) I suppose you'll want to . . .
Henry We'll just see what they're going to do. And I'll need his keys. Then you can run me up to the Dower House.
Dino Does he want something from there?
Henry No, dear. But I'm pretty sure he'll insist on being home tomorrow. So I'd be glad if you'd help me get the bed downstairs.
Dino Yes—but he shouldn't be alone . . .
Henry I'll stay there. Probably till Mrs Morris gets back. (*Looking at him*) Well, somebody's got to see him through.
Dino Whatever you say, love. But I don't reckon you'll stand it for more than a few days. You'll be glad to get back here.
Henry As a matter of fact, dear, I won't be staying here much longer.

Dino What do you mean?

Henry Well, you and Elsie should have the place to yourselves once you're married. And I can't stay at the shop because—did you know? Willie Flagg is moving in with Delia.

Dino Never!

Henry With or without benefit of clergy. Poor Merry hasn't been able to find out yet.

Dino But where're you——

Henry While you've been busy with your plans, I've been busy with mine. The documents were posted today.

Dino Henry, you're not going back to London?

Henry Oh no, dear. I couldn't run the business from there.

Dino (*blankly*) You haven't got a business.

Henry I've just bought one.

Dino What!

Henry A nice little general shop. Rather run down at the moment, but with considerable potential for expansion.

Dino You don't mean . . . ? Are you out of your mind?

Henry The bank didn't seem to think so.

Dino (*faintly*) You went to the bank?

Henry Where else does one go for money?

Dino You mean to say—at the present crippling rate—you're *borrowing* the money? What can you give them for security?

Henry They get the premises. And the goodwill. And thanks to your generosity, I may not have to borrow so much.

Dino But——

Henry Dino—do you know I think I've realized what Fabian was up to. He always was devious . . .

Dino How do you mean?

Henry If he'd left me rich, I would probably have drifted. I don't think he saw me as a sad old woman moving from hotel to hotel—living for an occasional bridge session and visits to the lending library . . .

Dino (*drily*) Or having a last fling with a bacon slicer.

Henry (*laughing*) Oh, that won't be for long. I shall put in a manager. I want to expand.

Dino (*resigned*) Expand.

Henry There's that big waste space behind the shop. I'm sure I could get planning permission. And don't worry about the bank. I've got a very good guarantor . . .

Dino A—Henry—not the *Admiral*!

Henry Good gracious, no. (*Pausing*) Though, come to think of it, he might take an interest. Mm. He could be very useful. He must be a mathematician——

Dino Henry——

Henry I mean—anyone who understands sextants—and binnacles—is hardly likely to boggle at a balance sheet——

Dino Henry! *Who is* this guarantor . . . ?

Henry (*vaguely*) Oh, just a friend. Rather an old and valued friend. (*Smiling*

Act III, Scene 2

to herself) I think there was a time when he wanted to marry me.
Dino Then it's a pity he doesn't marry you now, and stop all this nonsense.
Henry He can't very well do that, dear. I'm marrying the Admiral. (*She picks up her bag and case and moves* R)
Dino Henry ...!

She turns

Do you mean—the Admiral has *proposed* to you?
Henry Not exactly.
Dino What do you mean—not exactly? He either has or he hasn't. (*Suddenly*) You don't mean—you're not going to tell me *you* proposed to *him*!
Henry Certainly not. That would be most indelicate.
Dino (*losing patience*) HENRY!
Henry Yes?
Dino Has the Admiral—or has he not—asked you to marry him?
Henry (*gently*) Not yet, dear. But he will.

She goes out R

Dino Henry ...!

He rushes out after her

The door bangs. Suddenly the ominous groaning and gurgling is heard L. *The Lights begin to flicker more and more wildly. The sounds increase. The* CURTAIN *begins to descend slowly. As it touches the floor, there is a loud report off* L *and a puff of smoke drifts under the edge of the curtain into the auditorium*

CURTAIN

FURNITURE AND PROPERTY LIST

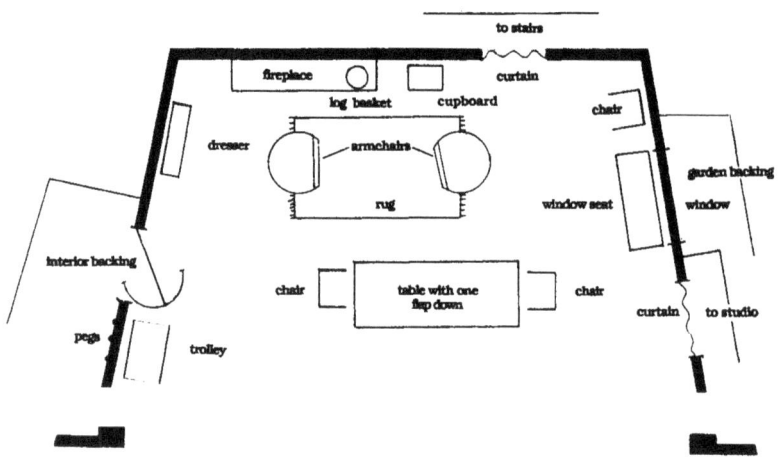

On stage: Fireplace. *On shelf above:* china Toby jug, plates, etc., penknife. *Under shelf:* line with 2 tea-towels, light sweater. *On hearth:* small pile of logs. *In hearth:* log fire
Brown upholstered armchair
Green velvet high-backed armchair
Small cupboard. *On it:* electric kettle (practical) with water, plugged into wall socket. *In cupboard:* tray with coffee filter jug, packet of ground coffee, 3 mugs, 3 spoons, small bottle of rum
Dresser. *On shelves:* untidy clutter of books, papers, drawing-pad. *On top:* 4 cups, 4 saucers, 6 glasses, bottle of wine, small bottle of brandy, transistor radio. *In drawer:* red and white checked tablecloth, star locket on gold chain in oblong box
Window seat. *on it:* cushions, valance, with slippers for Elsie underneath
Window curtains (*closed*)
Plug-in telephone with long lead on window sill
Trolley. *Above it:* wall mirror, row of hooks with 2 anoraks hanging
Gate-legged table with one flap down
3 upright chairs
2 floor-length curtains over entrance to studio and stairs
Rug

So What Do We Do About Henry?

Off stage: Suitcase **(Merry)**
Tray with 2 plates and pasties, 2 knives, 2 forks, 2 paper serviettes, 2 mugs, filter jug of coffee **(Elsie)**
2 small pictures **(Henry)**
Large framed painting of nude **(Henry)**
Large square portrait of Admiral **(Henry)**
Oblong brown paper parcel, large handbag **(Mrs Morris)**
White envelope **(Admiral)**
Brown paper **(Mrs Morris)**

Personal: **Henry:** handbag containing glasses, folded paper, postcard
Merry: wrist-watch
Dino: corkscrew, pencil in pocket
Admiral: wrist-watch

ACT II

Scene 1

Strike: Henry's handbag
Drawing-pad, pencil
Paper from hearth

Re-set: Telephone on window sill
Window curtains open

Off stage: Large box of books including copy of *Lysistrata* **(Mrs Morris)**
Small vacuum cleaner **(Elsie)**
Bamboo cane, flower pot with small plant **(Dino)**
Long piece of knotted string **(Elsie)**
Packet of letters, white envelope **(Merry)**
Cup of coffee **(Elsie)**
Cardigan **(Mrs Morris)**
Tray with 4 mugs and filter jug of coffee **(Elsie)**
Large plastic bowl, two towels **(Mrs Morris)**
Jacket **(Merry)**
Sketch-pad, pencil **(Dino)**

Personal: **Henry:** yellow duster, handkerchief and glasses in overall pocket
Merry: wrist-watch

Scene 2

Strike: Locket box

Off stage: Small suitcase **(Elsie)**
Small suitcase, handbag **(Henry)**
Portable typewriter, briefcase containing packet of photographs, car keys, notebook, pens, pencils, papers, handkerchief, plan of gallery **(Rupert)**
Green Harrods' box **(Dino)**

Personal: **Rupert:** glasses on chain round neck, wrist-watch

72 So What Do We Do About Henry?

ACT III

Scene 1

Strike: Typewriter, briefcase and all papers, etc. belonging to Rupert
Torn photographs from hearth
Line over fireplace

Re-set: Table fully extended c. *On it:* starched white cloth with lace border, 3 dessert plates, 3 linen napkins, bowl of fruit and nuts with nut crackers, 3 brandy glasses, decanter of brandy
Dresser tidied
Window curtains closed
Telephone on window seat
Refill kettle with water
Tray with mugs and coffee filter on cupboard

Set: New curtains at windows and entrances c and L
New covers on window seat
Painting on wall L beside curtain to stairs

Off stage: Silver tray with silver coffee-pot, cream jug, 3 small cups and saucers **(Mrs Morris)**
Hammer **(Delia)**
Sketch-pad, pencil **(Dino)**

Personal: **Henry:** brooch
Admiral: wrist-watch, handkerchief
Delia: hairnet

Scene 2

Strike: Dirty mug and glasses
Hammer
Sketch-pad, pencil

Re-set: Table c

Set: Duster for **Mrs Morris**

Off stage: Long legal envelope, small square envelope **(Henry)**
Large bundle of newspapers **(Merry)**
Newspaper **(Elsie)**
2 Fortnum & Mason carrier bags containing tins, packages, bottle of champagne, gift-wrapped box with gold bracelet, wrapped book, small brown paper bag containing emerald ring in case; Tesco carrier bag containing wads of notes in elastic bands **(Dino)**
Thin summer coat **(Elsie)**
Coil of rope, lengths of wood **(Dino)**
Spade **(Merry)**
Small glass of cloudy liquid **(Merry)**
Thick travelling rug **(Henry)**
Handbag, small suitcase **(Henry)**
Spade **(Dino)**

Personal: **Henry:** glasses
Admiral: handkerchief

LIGHTING PLOT

Property fittings required: log fire effect, light in studio off L
Interior. A cottage. The same scene throughout

ACT I Evening

To open: Full general lighting, fire effect on

Cue 1	**Dino:** "... a bit further on——" *Light clicks on off L*	(Page 9)
Cue 2	**Henry** puts log on fire *Increase fireglow*	(Page 13)
Cue 3	**Henry** exits R with tray *Lights flicker madly on and off*	(Page 18)
Cue 4	**Henry** appears in doorway R *Black-out, except for fireglow*	(Page 18)
Cue 5	Three loud clangs of hammer on metal *Snap up lighting, flickering wildly for a second, then returning to full*	(Page 18)

ACT II, SCENE 1 Morning

To open: Full general lighting, fire effect on, sun effect outside windows

| Cue 6 | **Henry** puts log on fire
 Increase fireglow | (Page 30) |

ACT II, SCENE 2 Morning

To open: Full general lighting

No cues

ACT III, SCENE 1 Late evening

To open: Full general lighting, fire effect on

Cue 7	**Delia** makes a faint mewing sound behind her hand *Repeat Cue 3*	(Page 51)
Cue 8	**Admiral:** "... what's happening!" *Vivid flash, then black-out*	(Page 51)
Cue 9	Three deafening metallic bangs off L *Snap up lights to full*	(Page 51)

Cue 10	**Dino** puts log on fire *Increase fireglow*	(Page 52)
Cue 11	**Henry:** "... while I just rinse this——" *Firelight catches* **Henry**	(Page 54)

ACT III, SCENE 2   Early evening

To open: Full general lighting

Cue 12	**Dino** rushes out after **Henry** *Lights flicker on and off wildly*	(Page 69)

EFFECTS PLOT

ACT I

Cue 1	**Elsie:** "I told you, Dino! Stop it!" *Loud knocking off R*	(Page 2)
Cue 2	**Elsie:** "You're not decent. I'll go——" *Repeat cue 1*	(Page 2)
Cue 3	**Elsie:** runs out R *Door slams, off R*	(Page 7)
Cue 4	**Dino:** "Henry—*please!*" *Crash off L*	(Page 11)
Cue 5	**Dino** goes off through curtain L *More bumps and crashes*	(Page 11)
Cue 6	**Dino:** "Watch out——!" *Thud*	(Page 11)
Cue 7	**Dino** hurries off R *Door slams, off R*	(Page 13)
Cue 8	**Henry** switches on radio *Soft background music*	(Page 13)
Cue 9	**Mrs Morris** switches off radio *Cut music*	(Page 13)
Cue 10	**Mrs Morris:** "Well, I'll get on." *Knock at door, off R*	(Page 15)
Cue 11	**Admiral** goes out R *Door closes off R*	(Page 17)
Cue 12	**Mrs Morris** goes out R *Door closes off R*	(Page 18)
Cue 13	**Henry exits** R with tray *Loud groaning and clanking of boiler—continue*	(Page 18)
Cue 14	**Henry** goes off through curtain L *Sounds continue, then 3 loud clangs of hammer on metal—clanking sounds cease*	(Page 18)

ACT II

Cue 15	As SCENE 1 opens *Vacuum cleaner off C*	(Page 21)
Cue 16	**Mrs Morris:** "Miss Henry!" (*2nd time*) *Cut vacuum*	(Page 21)

Cue 17	**Mrs Morris:** "Right you are." *Vacuum starts again—continue for a few seconds, then cut*	(Page 21)
Cue 18	**Henry** pushes up window *Seagulls, off—cut when **Henry** closes window*	(Page 22)
Cue 19	**Dino** tackles knots in string *Car approaches off* L	(Page 23)
Cue 20	**Elsie** pushes up window *Increase car noise; seagulls; car stops; fade seagulls slightly*	(Page 23)
Cue 21	**Elsie:** "Arthur! Hal-lo . . . ! *Child's voice calls "Hallo", off*	(Page 23)
Cue 22	**Elsie** shuts window *Cut seagull noise*	(Page 23)
Cue 23	**Dino** goes out L ***Arthur**'s voice as script page oo*	(Page 24)
Cue 24	**Elsie** pushes up window *Voices and seagulls off* L	(Page 25)
Cue 25	**Elsie:** ". . . giving the blessing——" *Fade voices and seagulls;* **Merry**'s *voice indistinguishable in distance*	(Page 25)
Cue 26	**Henry:** ". . . Dino's very good at——" *Child's shrill screaming and confusion of voices off* L *as pages 25–26*	(Page 25)
Cue 27	**Henry** crosses to window and looks out *Voices off as script page 30*	(Page 30)
Cue 28	**Henry** plugs in kettle *Car drives off in distance*	(Page 30)
Cue 29	**Elsie** runs out R *Door slams off* R	(Page 38)
Cue 30	**Dino** *(after pushing up window)* "ELSIE——!" *Seagull cries "Wak-wak-wak!"*	(Page 38)
Cue 31	**Dino:** "Right . . . !" *(2nd time)* *Telephone rings*	(Page 39)
Cue 32	**Rupert** goes off into studio *Pause, then small crash off* L	(Page 40)

ACT III

Cue 33	As SCENE 1 opens *Soft music in background from radio*	(Page 46)
Cue 34	**Henry:** ". . . which lifteth the waves thereof——" *Telephone rings*	(Page 49)
Cue 35	**Mrs Morris** collects everything on to tray *Car drives away, off* L	(Page 49)

So What Do We Do About Henry?

Cue 36	**Delia** makes a faint mewing sound behind her hand *Repeat Cue 13*	(Page 51)
Cue 37	Black-out; confused voices *3 deafening metallic bangs off* L	(Page 51)
Cue 38	**Dino** puts log on fire *Telephone rings*	(Page 52)
Cue 39	**Dino** plugs in kettle *Car drives away off* L	(Page 52)
Cue 40	As SCENE 2 opens *Typewriter off* C—*continue; pause, then telephone rings*	(Page 54)
Cue 41	**Mrs Morris:** "Miss Henry . . . !" (*2nd time*) *Cut typewriter*	(Page 55)
Cue 42	**Mrs Morris** returns to polishing table *Typewriter—continue for a moment then cut*	(Page 55)
Cue 43	**Mrs Morris** pushes up window *Seagulls, off*	(Page 55)
Cue 44	**Elsie:** "It's in the paper." *Car approaches off* R, *faintly*	(Page 57)
Cue 45	**Elsie** runs out R *Door slams off* R	(Page 60)
Cue 46	**Merry** collects up packets of money *Car approaches* L *at break-neck speed, then stops*	(Page 60)
Cue 47	**Admiral** (*off*): ". . . I'm standing by it——" *Splintering and crash off* R	(Page 62)
Cue 48	**Henry** pushes up window *Seagulls, becoming fainter*	(Page 62)
Cue 49	**Henry:** ". . . learn to enjoy it." *Ambulance bell off* L	(Page 66)
Cue 50	**Dino** and **Merry** ease the **Admiral** out R *Man's voice off* R *as page 67*	(Page 67)
Cue 51	**Henry** takes rug off C *Ambulance bell clangs off into distance*	(Page 67)
Cue 52	**Dino** rushes out after **Henry** *Door slams off* R, *then repeat cue 13, increasing in volume*	(Page 69)
Cue 53	As CURTAIN touches floor *Loud explosion off* L; *smoke drifts under edge of* CURTAIN	(Page 69)

MADE AND PRINTED IN GREAT BRITAIN BY
LATIMER TREND & COMPANY LTD PLYMOUTH
MADE IN ENGLAND

www.ingramcontent.com/pod-product-compliance
Ingram Content Group UK Ltd.
Pitfield, Milton Keynes, MK11 3LW, UK
UKHW021845210426
5322IPUK00022B/469